AF593626

SHEPHERD'S PIE

ANTHONY INGRAM, S.D.S.

SHEPHERD'S PIE

Farmer into Priest

FOREWORD BY
ROBERT SPEAIGHT

COLLINS
ST JAMES'S PLACE, LONDON
1971

William Collins Sons & Co Ltd

London · Glasgow · Sydney · Auckland

Toronto · Johannesburg

First published 1971

SBN 0 00 211799 1

Set in Monotype Bembo
Made and Printed in Great Britain by
William Collins Sons & Co Ltd Glasgow

CONTENTS

FOREWORD

This is the story of a vocation, and among the evidences for the existence of God the fact of vocation has always seemed to me one of the most irrefutable. Why this man more than another? Father Ingram tells his story with a straightforward, sincere, simplicity that carries a deep conviction. It is a story of hints, hesitations, doubts and prevailing purpose. The author is never controversial, and no more complicated than the average human being. He is, above all, honest and humble; and at a time when certain priests are so ready to tell us why they have deserted the altar it is a relief to be told of one who has never dreamed of turning his back upon it. Happy marriages are much more interesting than unhappy ones – a lesson that Father Ingram might well have learnt from Shakespeare's plays when he studied them at the Stratford-on-Avon Grammar School.

The Cotswold landscape – its architecture, farming, and rural crafts – forms the background to a boyhood in which the vocation to the priesthood planted its early seeds. The laws of nature and the unchanging rhythm of the seasons found their counterpart in the spiritual life. Father Ingram is something of a natural philosopher, as every good countryman should be. Often, in reading him, I was reminded of Gustave Thibon, the friend of Simone Weil – a philosopher more self-taught than Father Ingram, but rooted in the same realism. The reader will find here no exaggerated flights of fancy, no self-indulgent sentiment, no staking out of a position on the conservative or the progressive side in our present disputes. But he will recognize a man whom he would be grateful to have as his parish priest.

Robert Speaight

Chapter 1

HOOPS, GATES AND HURDLES

In a television interview, Artur Rubinstein said that he wondered if it was almost an indecent thing to say that he had been the happiest man that had ever lived. Looking back over the years of my priesthood, I feel very much as Rubinstein felt. It was my good fortune to be blessed with a happy home and loving parents and sisters. Though I lost my father, and one of my favourite sisters, at an early age, my mother has been a lasting source of strength throughout my whole life, and understanding friends, and their fine example, have been signposts pointing out the highway to happiness. In loving life I also love to the fullness of being. Life and love are two sides of the same coin.

My birthplace was situated at the foot of a lovely Cotswold hill, and the beauty of the Cotswolds forms the background of my life. Since I had been born in love and happiness, and rightly fostered on these all-important realities of living, it was to take me some years before the circle of my loving was to widen out to embrace others. Acquiring a catholicity of loving sums up the main object of the education of a child.

There are in one's early memories certain very localized and time-circumscribed events that tend to linger in the memory. Usually these are associated with dramatic incidents in the family circle. My first vivid remembrance is centred round a red carpet. I was about two years old at the time; the carpet had been my playground. It was difficult to believe that it could be so transformed when rolled up and laid like a gigantic sausage at my feet. The reason for this was that it was being stacked with the rest of our furniture in a horse-drawn van that was taking us to our new home at the Old Wharf.

We moved into the Old Wharf as the 1914 war was starting and, hearing so much talk about the war and the Wharf, I confused the two in my mind and took it for granted that we were going off to the war. Our new home had originally been an inn and wharf for the horse-drawn railway that was built to connect the canal at Stratford-on-Avon with the corn-growing area of the Cotswolds. It had not been a financial success and both the inn and the wharf had been closed down for some time before we moved there. Remnants of this railway can still be seen at Stratford-on-Avon.

Our house was large and rather gaunt for a child, and its charm lay in the collection of outbuildings. There was a row of stables, store sheds and a bakehouse. This had a large brick oven and once a week a woman came from the village to help my mother make our bread. The flour was milled at a nearby water-mill on the River Stour; the oven was heated by inserting several faggots of twigs and then setting them on fire. Later, the wood ash was raked out and the bread baked on the hot firebricks of the floor of the oven. The loaves were put in on a long-handled wooden shovel. I can still recapture the warm fragrance of that bakehouse. The brown bread was delicious and as different from modern soggy steam-baked bread as wine is from water.

One of the buildings had been built as a bowling-alley. It was narrow and long and one end and side were open to the weather. The floor was made of beaten clay, and when we took over the skittle pit was still there. All the buildings were of honeyed Cotswold stone, with the exception of one large red-brick construction, a dance-hall which had an excellent wooden floor. A deep well stood outside our back door and all our water supply had to be pumped by hand.

My earliest memories are largely centred round these outbuildings. Had they been empty they might have scared a small child, but they were occupied by busy craftsmen. There is a natural joy in watching men doing manual work, and this is all the greater when they are experts at their trade, and these men were doing extraordinary things in wood by using the most primitive of tools and home-made equipment. It was fascinating to sit watching their deft fingers at work and listening while they sang folk songs, or the latest music-hall hit, or told tales of village folklore and gossip. Even as they talked or sang, their hands played rings round their work, like a talented beat-group drummer of today.

My family had been wood hoop makers for generations. This is a country craft that is now almost extinct. The work was highly skilled and took several years to learn. The hoops were gigantic things up to twenty feet in circumference and were used for making the large barrels in which raw cotton was shipped to Manchester. Iron hoops were too heavy for this purpose and, as yet, light alloy hoops had not been invented. It required considerable skill to split the long ash poles into quarter or sixth sections, the natural tendency of the wood being to split off at a tangent. The rough centres were then hacked off with a splitting axe. Afterwards the long lengths of poles were cramped into a home-made wooden vice and shaved down into smoothly shaped hoops. When finished, they were heated in a long wooden box in which steam was circulating until they were pliable enough to bend. This was done in a wooden frame shaped rather like a rocking-horse. Only the finest ash poles could be used for making hoops and they had to be of exactly ten years' growth. Poles that were too rough for hoops were made into gates, hurdles, ladders, stakes and rick-pegs, so that nothing was wasted.

Each year we bought a wagonload of pears and, to my delight, a man would arrive with a cider press and crush them into perry. This made a pleasant drink which was not so rough on the tongue as cider. We had a vast cellar, dating from the days when the Old Wharf was an inn; it made an excellent storage place for the perry. When farmers came to buy our gates and hurdles it was customary to offer them a jug of perry, and it was my job to fetch it for them. Some arrived in dirty carts and wore ragged clothing, while others were smartly dressed and came in gaily painted gigs with prancing horses. A few drove weird and wonderful motors that would now merit pride of place in an Old Crocks' rally.

One of them was a wealthy self-made man who could neither read nor write. He was like G. K. Chesterton in bulk and had a huge whisky-red nose that was covered with warts. We children would cluster round him in rapt attention. He may have been flattered by this childish interest, but the reason behind it was that we were competing with each other to see who could count the largest number of his warts.

Some of the farmers followed an age-old tradition and enjoyed spending a long time haggling over the prices. The haggling followed a set ritual which both parties accepted and carried out according to definite rules. They pitted their wits against each other and argued over a shilling as though they were on the floor of the Stock Exchange. The process of bargaining often ended in compromise, and the farmers would be so pleased at having saved a few pence that sometimes they would hand me this change as a tip for fetching the perry.

When the farmers brought their rosy-cheeked children along with them it was my joy to take them on a grand tour of the outbuildings. The dance-hall I kept as the finale, and I would stop at the entrance and make a special point of asking permission before entering, which effectively impressed on my guests the importance of the occasion. The pungent smell of wood shavings, the boiler and the long steam box, the wooden vices and the deft hands of the busy workmen made a vivid impression on the small children.

The wood shavings made excellent fire-lighters and we sold them by the sackful to the villagers for a few pence. These pennies were my pocket-money and, as trade tended to vary considerably, I soon learned the value of keeping strict control over my spending.

The climax of the year came in the late spring when we hauled home the loads of ash poles on heavy timber wagons drawn by teams of horses. Gangs of men had worked in the woods throughout the winter months cutting and stacking the poles and making faggots out of the brushwood. Sometimes my father took me with him when he was visiting the men and I have happy memories of the rolling hills, soft dews and the fragrance, as we plunged our way through undergrowth and bushes. A startled wood-pigeon would suddenly crash its way through the branches above us and my heart would leap with excitement, and lively red squirrels gave us a free circus exhibition as they jumped from branch to branch high up in the trees.

Often the woods were situated in remote valleys among the hills and were almost inaccessible to our timber wagons. As soon as the ground was dry, we hired teams of horses from the local farmers to bring home the ash poles that had been stacked on the edge of the woods. Each team of horses had its own carter and they would vie with each other in polishing the brasses and grooming the horses. Cart-horses are massive yet elegant creatures, and four of them in a row can give an impression of immense power as they stamp their feet and blow clouds of steam from their nostrils on a frosty morning. Usually we had to negotiate bogs and ditches. The method we used, employed by my father while in the Royal Engineers, was to take faggots of brushwood and lay them in the ditches. These allowed the water to flow through and gave ample support to the heaviest loads.

One incident stands out in my memory. Several loads of poles had to be transported down a rough farm-track, then pass through a very narrow gateway at the bottom of the valley, and finally be hauled up a muddy hill on the opposite side. Four teams of horses were linked together in one long line of sixteen, and each had its own carter. The wagons were driven at breakneck speed down the slope, with only inches to spare as they shot through the gateway, and, with the cracking of whips and shouts of encouragement from the carters, the sweating horses heaved and strained as they galloped through the mud up the steep hill on the other side. No cowboy film will ever convey the drama of that scene, and I can still hear the ringing shouts of those carters as they skilfully guided their horses through the narrow gateway.

The meetings of the local hunt added colour and excitement to village life. Many of us followed on foot, and by keeping to the hilltops we had a splendid view of the horsemen in the valleys below. As a boy, I saw only the beauty and excitement of the chase, for the sight of red-coated horsemen and dappled hounds, leaping over hedges and stone walls, is a spectacle of great beauty. It was not until my early teens that I saw something of the more brutal side of this sport. It was the cub-hunting season and, instead of a fox, the hounds gave chase to a badger. The badger fought and crashed its way through the undergrowth, hounds snarled and yelped, horsemen dismounted and joined in the chase. Eventually the badger was cornered in a clearing in the woods where it stood, majestically at bay, in the centre of a circle of snapping hounds. Being a brave fighter, it easily kept the hounds off, so that they had to be whipped on by the son of the master of the hounds. It was a revolting sight as the hounds slowly tore the badger into pieces and its entrails were dragged out by the yard as it still kept on fighting.

Filled with sick anger at this wanton cruelty, I had a strong urge to wade in and try to stop the fight, but was far too afraid to make a move. It was not the fear of getting hurt, but rather of what the rest of the villagers might think and say. I felt shamed and disgusted, not only at the brutality but also by my cowardice. This sense of failure helped me to realize that it is one thing to have high ideals, but quite another matter when one has to pay the cost of these ideals.

Sunday was then indeed a day of rest, for country people used to work a twelve-hour day and, after finishing, many of them would walk quite a distance to cultivate their plot of land. Our life tended to revolve round Sunday. The

Catholic faith had been kept alive in the remote country areas by the few landed families who could afford to pay the heavy fines imposed during the penal times for non-attendance at the State church. We were fortunate in that the Howard family owned a country estate, some three miles from our home, and maintained a chaplain. During my boyhood, the Berkeley family rented this estate and kept a chaplain in residence. Indeed, we had a succession of chaplains, for either they were old and semi-retired, or young and invalids, so no one stayed for very long. The chapel stood on a hill a thousand feet above sea-level. Before the advent of radio and television, Sunday walks were an integral part of country life, and during the summer months we would often walk to the chapel for evening service, or go for long walks in the hills.

The chapel was ugly and built in imitation Renaissance style which jarred with the elegance of traditional Cotswold architecture. A cousin of mine played the harmonium and, as her repertoire was extremely limited, we were brought up on a meagre diet of her favourite hymns, or rather of my aunt's favourite hymns, for she it was who called the tune. As we paid bench rent to supplement the chaplain's small income, we sat in the same places every Sunday. A rotund little man, whose pate was as smooth as a Swiss lake, sat in front of me; his fat neck was a mass of wrinkles which I used to count during the long sermons. These were the days when a half-hour's sermon was considered short. The fat man's wife was a jolly little woman with a smile as large as her warm heart. Sometimes, when my mother went out shopping, she left me at this woman's cottage and I have happy memories of her kindness to me. Opposite us were two farmers and their families; one, tall and thin with a sad face, who had a domineering wife and lanky children; the other, gentle and kindly with the calm eyes of a man who tends animals with a loving heart. His wife reminded me of a toasted chestnut on a hob; she had bright red cheeks and small smiling eyes, and was as quick as a squirrel in her movements.

Our congregation differed considerably in their home backgrounds, ranging from the Berkeleys to casual labourers, but the moment we entered the chapel we all became one family without any distinctions, and there was a sense of complete peace and prayerfulness that had to be experienced to be believed. Belloc, in his *Path to Rome*, describes the sense of peace and calm that he experienced when attending early morning mass in a small Alpine village, and says that this peace of the mass put him in the right frame of mind for the rest of the day. In the same way, our Sunday mass put us in the right mood for the rest of the week and gave richness and purpose to all that we did. Some people think that Catholics attend mass out of fear of offending God and the Church, but Catholics know all the peace and relaxation of body, as well as of soul, that the Sunday mass brings to their daily life.

The walk to our chapel was a haphazard affair. We arrived in scattered groups and were too breathless from climbing the steep hill for conversation. The return journey was quite different, for we emerged in a cluster and soon the women were deep in conversation, while the men spent some moments lighting up their clay pipes and sorting themselves out into accepted groups. Always the first topic of debate would be the sermon; these discussions were often more interesting than the sermon itself, and they left a vivid impression on my mind. Radio and television had not yet made any impact on country life and, perhaps because of this, there was a high standard of debate and of conversation. In any case, the men of the Cotswold Hills tend to be very independent in outlook, a trait that may still be observed today in the Cotswold inns. As writers such as H. V. Morton and Harold Massingham have recorded, some of the vocabulary of their dialect dates back to the time of Shakespeare.

Much later, after visiting the various holy places of Greece and Crete, I came to wonder whether such debates as those outside our chapel may not have taken place among the worshippers of ancient Crete and Greece as they made their way home from their temples, and whether such debates may not have been at the origin of the wealth of Grecian thought which later became the corner-stone on which the whole of Christian philosophy was to be built. There is a great depth of wisdom to be found among people who work in solitude or ply a craft. Perhaps the long hours spent in plodding behind a plough, or tending sheep on remote and bleak hills, encourage reflection. Is it not perhaps because so much of our present-day thinking is done for us by journalists, who have to do their thinking at great speed in order to meet a dead-line, and because we live in an age in which the emphasis is placed on quantity rather than quality, that today we tend to be a generation of talkers rather than of thinkers?

As a boy, I took my Catholic faith very much for granted, although I was aware that we were a race apart. Not that we formed a ghetto, but there tended to be some rivalry and suspicion between the various religious bodies in the village. Other people may probably have thought of Catholics as foreigners, but we were very conscious of the fact that we had inherited the age-old traditions of Catholic

England and, in our eyes, it was the other religions that had ousted us from our rightful inheritance.

The view from my bedroom window was graced by the distant outline of a clump of trees that crown Brailes Hill. Mass was said in this village right through the penal times, and this was the home of the first vicar-apostolic in England after the Reformation.

We had a two-mile walk to our village school, and sometimes I lagged behind my sisters and dodged into a cottage where a gaunt old man lived who had previously worked for my father. He was a Quaker and was deeply religious. In one sense he taught me more about the Bible than the whole staff of the Biblical Institute in Rome did in later years. He would welcome me with the delight that old age sometimes shows to children, and while he boiled his kettle and made tea he would yarn about his life's experiences. Then, as the clock struck eleven, he would walk over to the huge family Bible that stood in a place of honour near his cottage window and, with great solemnity, would take out his steel-rimmed glasses, clean them with his red spotted handkerchief, clear his throat and read out the passage for the day. It was not what he read but the loving reverence with which he read it that made a lasting impression on me. I owe part of my vocation as a priest to this dear old man, and I pray God that he is now rejoicing among the angels, for when on this earth he was as holy and innocent as an angel.

My mother came from a staunch Protestant family and when she became a Catholic, in her early teens, she was excluded from her home. My father's family had been loyal Catholics through the difficult era of the Reformation and the ensuing penal times. It was impressive to see him at his prayers. He would kneel down beside us as we said our night prayers and join in them with such sincerity that he seemed one of us. He was a good athlete and an all-round sportsman, and I thought of him as being all-powerful, but the fact that he could still kneel down and ask for help from a Being greater than himself made a strong bridge between us.

Chapter 2

THE VILLAGE AND THE TOWN

IT used to be the custom for children to be told that their First Communion day would be the happiest day of their lives. As a child, I could not accept this as there were days in my life that seemed to me to have been far happier, but, looking back on that day, I realize that even if it was not the happiest day of my childhood, it was nevertheless a very happy day.

The whole of our small Catholic community shared in the celebration. Farmers lent their gaily painted wagons and their finest horses to bring us to the chapel. The carters spent hours grooming their horses, plaiting their tails with brightly coloured ribbons and polishing the brasses that hung on the leather harnesses. The wagons were masterpieces of the painter's art, the spokes of the wheels and the sides of the wagon were picked out in intricate designs such as one sometimes sees on Romany caravans. The wheelwrights and coachbuilders who made and painted these wagons were the forerunners of the coachbuilders of our present-day limousines.

To ride in a wagon behind a heavy carthorse is quite an experience. The wagon creaks and groans as the big horse sways and pulls in the shafts; it is like cresting the waves in an old sailing ship. Holding a wooden plough behind a team of heaving horses is a similar sort of experience.

Normally we left the chapel by passing through the back entrance of the mansion, but on this day we turned into the house where the Berkeley family had prepared a special breakfast for all of us. It was something of a thrill to enter the mansion for the first time, but once inside the big and lofty rooms I felt frightened by their size and coldness and was much happier when we reached the servants' hall in the basement. But Georgian houses tell eloquently the story of the social injustices of their times. One has only to see the dark and gloomy basements and cold attics in which the underpaid servants had to live and work to know what the lives of the staff were like. This basement was no exception, but it was redeemed by the friendly, smiling faces of the servants who had gone to great pains to make this breakfast worthy of the occasion. In fact, home-cured bacon and fresh eggs were our staple diet, yet the unfamiliar setting made this breakfast seem as the nectar of the gods. To be truthful, I have no distinct memory of my First Communion as such, but only of the tempting smell of bacon and eggs.

After breakfast we all trooped down to visit the old chaplain in his cottage in the woods. He was a gentle old man with snow-white hair, and all of us were very much at ease with him. His study had a fusty smell of dampness and his books and papers were scattered on every available piece of furniture. All went well until we visited his outside water-closet. This held unknown wonders for us as it was the only toilet in the village fitted with a water flush system. Stories of this amazing thing had been handed down from child to child and we were all agog to see it. We had planned things so that some of us kept the old priest chatting while others stole out to inspect the curiosity. When my turn came I gave the chain a hefty pull and the resulting sudden rush of water and the gurgling of the tank filled me with such terror that I fled in panic. In the afternoon we played games on the lawn and I won first prize for pulling the ugliest face.

Cycles played an important part in country life; they were passports to freedom. My first ride was not entirely successful. One day, when pushing my mother's cycle home from the repair shop, I tried to ride it. Within seconds I found myself flying through the air with the ease of a swallow on the wing, until I ended up in the mud of the village pond at the foot of the hill. Cars were very rare and unreliable and few could master the Cotswold Hills without a breakdown. Most of the transport was by horse or railway. Farmers and tradespeople travelled by pony and trap, and if the farmer got drunk at the market he could sleep it off in his trap while the pony brought him back home safely.

Twice a week the local carrier journeyed to Stratford-on-Avon to do the shopping for the villagers. He had a wonderful memory and was able to buy dozens of small items for different people without having to write them down. His covered wagon was big and lumbering and held over a dozen people. In summer it was a pleasant drive, but in winter it was freezing cold and one needed heavy coats and rugs to keep warm.

Only the main road from Stratford to London was tarred; the others were surfaced with Cotswold stone which was rolled into position by a heavy steam-roller. They were a rich golden colour and showed up very clearly in the dark. Carriage lamps of brass were lit by candles and were adjusted by strong springs fitted inside the holders. Cycle lamps were lit by oil and they frequently blew out in the wind. The road-menders spent their winter months in breaking up the heaps of stones by the roadside. For this they used long-handled hammers with very small heads; they worked at great speed. Our local road-mender was the village philosopher. He was a thoughtful, gentle character, and most folk stopped for a chat with him for his advice was greatly valued and he never betrayed a confidence.

The village shop, crammed with every imaginable object, was full of exciting and aromatic smells. Groceries were kept in drawers or large bags and were weighed out on a pair of swinging scales and then wrapped in stiff blue paper. I used to stand in silent awe when the old lady behind the counter performed a minor miracle before my eyes as she deftly transformed a flat piece of paper into a sugar bag. Bunches of candles were hung by their long wicks from the rafters and large tins of paraffin stood by the doorway. There was no electricity or gas in the village so we depended on paraffin lamps and candles for light. Going to bed by candle-light can be much more attractive than it sounds, for there is something very restful and soothing in the softness of the light, and the act of blowing out a candle has a finality about it that heralds the repose of sleep. It is interesting to observe how the more imaginative members of a generation re-discover the simple joys of an earlier one: dining out by candle-light can still add charm to an expensive meal.

One could buy almost anything at our village shop. There were coils of rope, balls of string, stationery, pots and pans, gleaming buckets, brooms, brushes, mops, and tools of every description. Propped on their edges were smoothly shaped wooden yokes for carrying two buckets of water from the village wells. Corduroy trousers were piled in heaps along with small leather straps for hitching them up in wet weather. It was then considered effeminate for men to wear shoes, and rows of boots stood on a long narrow bench. There were hob-nailed heavy boots for work, and light boots for Sunday, and boots for country women and children which had soft uppers and were fastened with buttons. It was like playing a game of hide-and-seek to help the old lady search out her treasures, a kind of self-service years ahead of its time.

Some of the villagers were characters worthy of Dickens or Shakespeare. The local builder was an agnostic and self-educated. He had a phenomenal memory and delighted in quoting long passages from the Bible at the vicar. He had a terrible temper. It was a standing joke in the village that whenever he mowed his orchard for hay-making it would begin to rain. One year he got so furious about this that he dashed out in the pouring rain and began to water the hay with his watering-can.

Sam Bennett was another colourful character. He was a stocky little man who was always singing as he jogged along with his pony and trolley, the trolley usually crowded with a group of happy, singing children, for he was a sort of Pied Piper and wherever he went the children would flock after him. He was the village carrier and had a thriving fruit business as well. On the green outside his house he erected a maypole for he was an enthusiastic morris-dancer. He did much to help Cecil Sharpe in his research work on folk songs. For many years he organized the morris-dancing at Stratford-on-Avon for the Shakespeare birthday celebrations, and several times he danced before royalty. He played his fiddle by ear and was usually out of tune, but he made up for this with his powerful lungs and his infectious enthusiasm. Until he was nearly eighty he danced the Broom dance with a verve and ecstasy that was a delight to behold. When he was seventy-five he challenged another old man to a race in mowing an acre of grass by scythe.

Another of our neighbours, George Hanse, was a man of many accomplishments. For years he was shepherd to a prize-winning flock of Cotswold sheep. Cotswold sheep were quite different from the more common Welsh sheep one sees today, and very few of them now survive. They were big animals and had large black faces. George had nearly four hundred sheep in his flock and, being a lay preacher, he named them all after Old Testament characters. Like all good shepherds, he knew each one of his sheep by name, although to an outsider they all seemed alike. Hanse was a big man and wore a bushy black beard which contrasted with his twinkling blue eyes, set under enormous eyebrows. He was very clever with his fingers, and when he retired from being a shepherd he worked for us for some time making hurdles. He was chosen by the BBC to introduce the first broadcast made by George V, and did this most successfully. Although he was the village pig-killer, he loved all animals and he acted as an unqualified veterinary surgeon in tending sick animals.

Pig-killing was an epic event in a country boy's life, for it had all the drama of a Greek tragedy. The pig-killer would arrive carrying his bench for killing on his shoulders and wearing a blue striped apron and a leather belt that had a huge brass buckle and a leather pouch in which were a row of sharp knives. On arrival, he would take out his knives and sharpen them on his belt in a way that sent shivers down my spine. A group of men would advance on the pigsty like members of a classical chorus and then bring out the pig on a cord. They held it on the bench while the pig-killer severed its main artery. Death was immediate. Country men, who tend animals for their living, are usually very kind to them. They will spend sleepless nights in caring for sick animals, and often there develops a strong bond of affection between man and beast.

As soon as the pig was dead we lit a straw fire and singed off the bristles and then the pig was expertly cut up into various joints. Nothing was wasted. Even the intestines were thoroughly cleaned and then twisted and cooked into what we called chitterlings. These were very tasty. It was customary to present one's friends with joints of fresh meat, and when they killed their pigs they would return the compliment. The main joints were salted down in a shallow pig-trough; salt played an essential part in preserving meat before the coming of refrigeration. This is why it was so expensive and important in former times; indeed, the word 'salary' is derived from the Latin word for 'salt'. This also explains the point of the Gospel story about salt not losing its savour. It is not so much that salt adds flavour to food, but rather that it is essential in preventing it from going rotten.

Harvesting was a community exercise in the village. Some of the men worked part-time for the bigger farmers, while in their free time they cultivated their own plot of land. They harvested their crops by hand and whole families clubbed together to help get in the crops. This was a survival from Saxon days when land was divided into small and scattered sections, so that all had their fair share of good and bad land.

The men cut the corn with fagging hooks, the corn being held in position with a crooked stick and then rolled into a sheaf against the side of their leg. Sometimes I went along with a group of families and helped the other children and women pull out handfuls of straw which was then twisted into binding for fastening the sheaves. It was back-aching work and the rough straw cut one's fingers, but there was a sense of fun and excitement that made up for all this. When the women helped in cutting they used a lightweight sickle that had a serrated edge which they used in a saw-like action. We children worked all day for the promise of a ride when the corn was harvested. Custom decreed that the church bells must ring three times before the stacked corn was dry enough to gather.

I remember seeing two old men threshing their corn with flails. These were made out of heavy sticks fastened together with leather thongs. They grasped one of the sticks and used it as a handle, while the other was swung round their heads and brought down flat on the heads of the corn that was laid out on the stone flags of the barn floor. After this they waited for a windy day and then winnowed the corn by opening up the barn doors and tossing the corn and husks into the breeze, the light husks being blown to one side.

We had a wealth of country legends that had been handed down from generation to generation in much the same way as the early forms of the Bible were handed down. Elaborate yarns about people long since dead had a definite word-form and pattern that never varied in the telling. We children listened eagerly to the old people telling these stories. Although we knew them off by heart it was considered bad form not to pretend that one was hearing the story for the first time. The amusing thing was that if the storyteller stumbled over a word one was allowed to prompt him, *sotto voce*, and the storyteller would continue as though he had not been prompted. Storytelling such as this is a survival of the drama forms that date back to pre-alphabet times.

A typical yarn concerned a couple who had lived in the

last century. Joe Hubard stayed at home looking after his widowed mother until her death, and he was middle-aged when she died. He then wished to get married but was far too shy to ask any of the village girls to marry him, so he confided in the local carrier who promised to look out for a possible wife for him while on his rounds. Eventually, the carrier heard of a middle-aged woman who was looking for a husband, and it was arranged that the two should meet halfway between their villages. The carrier could not resist telling some of the village wags about the forthcoming meeting and they hid behind a hedge to see what happened. Shy Joe Hubard walked straight up to the woman and asked: 'Be you Ann Dollidge?' She answered: 'I be.' Without any further words being spoken they clasped hands and walked straight off to the vicar to put up the banns of their marriage. Tradition has it that they were the happiest married couple in the village.

Few families could afford to buy a daily paper and, anyway, in their eyes the local paper published at Evesham was far more important than the national press. It was avidly read by everyone and then hotly discussed. It was made up of various items of news sent in by any local worthy who could spell correctly. Because of that it had a direct contact with the people and their problems and played an important part in country life and activities. Births, deaths and marriages formed the backbone of the copy. When a person died his whole life's story would be discussed for months afterwards, and choice episodes would be handed on to add to the riches of village folklore.

As soon as I was old enough to ride a cycle I left the village school and went with my sisters to attend the convent school at Chipping Campden, which was six miles away on the other side of a thousand-foot-high Cotswold hill. We cycled over on the Sunday evening and boarded out until the following Friday night. I lodged in a cottage near the Catholic church where I was treated as one of the family. It was a new experience for me to be free to attend daily mass. Quite a number of people would be present, and the nuns would kneel in their benches so still and quiet that they looked like carved figures on medieval tombs. One man made a lasting impression on me. He was a retired business-man, a convert, and said to be a millionaire. He was tall and stately, but what impressed me was the respectful way in which he genuflected before the Blessed Sacrament. It was a sermon without words. I still treasure the memory of the peace and tranquillity of those early morning masses at Chipping Campden.

The town is one of the loveliest in England, which is saying a great deal. It nestles among the hills, and its fine perpendicular church tower can be seen for miles around. The houses in the High Street are built of that honey-coloured sandstone which reminded H. V. Morton of bottled sunshine, and the delicate stone-mullioned windows, the tall gabled roofs and the graceful rounded arches of the old market-hall combine to make it one of the most attractive streets I have ever seen. It had an air of peace and tranquillity that bordered on prayerfulness and I felt immediately at home there.

Chapter 3

FARM-HAND AND SCHOLAR

IN 1923 events happened which were to have a profound effect on my future and which indirectly prepared the way for my vocation to the priesthood. I was the youngest of four children and the only boy in the family. I loved all my sisters, but I had a special relationship with my sister Mary; she seemed able to read my inmost thoughts and the bond of sympathy between us was very close. She had such a happy disposition that everybody loved her. One morning she overslept and my parents sent me to wake her. I went into her room to find her sitting up in bed with a high fever. She looked penetratingly at me out of a sea of pain. It was an extraordinary glance and only lasted for a few seconds, yet I was sure that she was saying 'Goodbye'. I fled from the room in panic and went weeping to the breakfast table, crying that Mary was going to die. My parents did their best to calm my fears, but within six months she was dead. When she died I was at school. When the nuns called me out of the classroom into the convent parlour I sensed their embarrassment: I knew that they were trying to prepare me for the bad news. While they were searching for apt words I told them quietly that my sister was dead. My calmness shook them, but I was so convinced that this would happen that I accepted her death as inevitable, and yet with her death one half of me seemed to die.

A few months after this my father too died. The loss of my sister had partly prepared me for the shock of his death. He had been ill ever since returning home after four years of fighting during the 1914–18 war, in which he had suffered gas-poisoning before masks were issued to the troops. One night I heard a strange noise and rushed into his room to see him choking to death in my mother's arms from a severe haemorrhage. In spite of the horror of the moment my mother thought of my feelings and told me to run and fetch my aunt, but I knew that this was only an excuse to get me out of the way. At three in the morning I banged at my aunt's door and as she opened it I told her that my father was dead, which indeed proved to be true. His funeral, so simple and dignified, made a deep impression on me. Some of the local bell-ringers had worked for him for years and they rang a muffled peal. The soft thud of the leather muffles on the bells seemed to comfort me in my misery, much more than words could. The coffin was carried on a timber carriage which was draped with the Union Jack, and the last post was sounded over his grave. That evening our dog ran away from home and after a search we found him guarding the grave which he refused to leave until I coaxed him home. This same dog used to walk two miles to wait for me on my way home from school. Without any prompting from anyone, he did this only on the Friday night which was when I returned.

For some months I was too numbed with the shock of my double loss to realize fully what had happened. Then things built up into a crisis and I ran away from school. I was so upset that the family doctor was called in who ordered a complete break from school until it was time for me to start at Stratford-on-Avon Grammar School in the autumn. He was a wise man for those months in the fresh air helped to build me up and enabled me to come to terms with the past.

Death is a shocking thing for those who are left behind, and no attempts to rationalize it can lessen the shock, no matter how much one attempts to shake it off, for the bitterness clings on. Unhappy as I was, I was not morbid, for living in close contact with nature had taught me to accept death as an inevitable fact in life's cycle. Moreover, my Catholic faith convinced me that my loved ones had entered into the fullness of life in eternity, so, although the sense of loss was very painful, there was at the same time a sensation of being closer to them than ever before. Catholics call this the communion of saints. It is a thing that has to be experienced to be understood.

Death is an evil thing, and the pain and suffering that it brings in its wake are evil things; nevertheless, such sorrows, if accepted in faith and trust, can bring forth good fruit in ways not fully understood at the time. In my case, my vocation to the priesthood was to come about largely because of my father's death. Had he lived I would have gone to a Catholic boarding-school and, such are the quirks of fate, it is doubtful if at a Catholic school I would have developed a vocation as I did at a non-Catholic one.

My mother was to need much courage in the years that followed for, from the financial point of view, disaster piled upon disaster. She was an excellent businesswoman and during the years from 1914 to 1918, when my father was away, she had run the family business and brought up four small children. After his death she was to need plenty of skill to keep things going while we children were being educated. Gradually she realized that, owing to the discovery of light alloys during the war, the old craft of wood hoop-making was coming to an end. This was a terrible blow. We had large stocks of hoops and it was some time before our business friends were able to take them off our hands at a nominal price. After this we carried on with the gate and hurdle business, but there were not sufficient profits to make it worth while, so as soon as our oldest employees had retired, we closed down. This was very sad for me as I loved the wood hoop trade and would have liked nothing better than to have carried on with it.

Like many country business people we had always done some farming as a side-line and had recently begun to specialize in pig-farming. When my father died we had a large stock of fat pigs due for the market, but were unable to move them owing to the outbreak of foot-and-mouth disease. We had to keep them for some months, during which time it cost us pounds to feed them.

My mother knew nothing about farming, but now our only hope of survival was to increase our farming activities. After a few unsuccessful attempts, she was fortunate in finding a farm manager who proved to be an expert. He had a natural gift with animals and this left my mother free to attend to the business side of things. For some years it was a struggle to make ends meet for this was the time of the post-war depression, and farming was badly hit by the slump. It meant that I had to spend my weekends and holidays in helping out on our small farm. Some jobs, such as hoeing crops by hand, could be very monotonous and back-breaking, though it was an experience that was to be invaluable to me in my future work as a priest.

We rented some of our land from the local county council and, in spite of these difficult times, my mother ended up by winning the first prize for a small farm in the county. She encouraged our farm manager to save part of his wages so that, when we eventually sold out, he would be able to take over part of our stock and start farming on his own. In spite of the hard work these were happy days, for there is a paradox in the heart of man in that he is never happier than when he is stretched to the full.

My sisters were away at a boarding-school and, as it was out of the question for me to leave home, it was arranged that I should attend Stratford-on-Avon Grammar School as a day boy. The six years I spent there were some of the happiest of my life, which is saying a great deal. The teaching staff were very friendly and liberal-minded, and the fact that I was the only Catholic boy in the school never made the slightest difference in their attitude towards me. The present-day tolerance and ecumenical understanding between the various denominations in this country is a hopeful sign for future unity, but I had practical experience of it half a century ago.

The time that I spent at this school laid the foundations of my vocation to the priesthood, because I loved the school, its staff and my school-mates, and as time passed by I longed to see this historic old school restored to its Catholic inheritance. The school badge was a simple Greek cross, the emblem of the old Guild of the Holy Cross, and this acted as a challenge to me in my thoughts on the priesthood.

One of the main aims of education should be to open up the catholicity of our love and understanding of other people, places and things. Most of the stages towards growth in maturity in my life have focused round a journey. My first remembered journey, when we moved to the Old Wharf, then the wagon journey to receive Holy Communion, and the brief but exhilarating journey on my mother's cycle into the village pond, and now the journey to Stratford-on-Avon.

For the first four miles I cycled along with the local vicar's son and a farmer's son. We then caught the Shipston to Stratford bus for the remainder of the ten-mile journey. The bus had solid tyres and an open top deck with wooden seats. The driver was a jolly Pickwickian type who sat in front exposed to the weather. Everybody knew him and liked him and would shout their greetings as we passed by, so that our journey had the nature of a triumphant procession. The passengers talked to each other as they still do in countries such as Italy and Greece.

The climax of the journey came as we crossed over Clopton bridge into Stratford. If any person wishes to enter into the mind and soul of Shakespeare, he would do well to leave his car on the London side of the Avon and then cross the bridge on foot. It is a significant fact that Shakespeare has been called 'the swan of Avon'. The river at this point has a quiet calm and peace that puts one into the right frame of mind to appreciate the gentle charm of Stratford and its lovely half-timbered buildings, of which sufficient remain to give us an insight into its beauty in Shakespeare's day.

All running water is fascinating, but here the waters of the Avon have a poetry all of their own. I wonder how much Shakespeare owed to rivers such as the Avon and the Thames, for the Thames was equally lovely in his day and had not yet been ruined by drab warehouses and unimaginative buildings and enclosures.

How much do artists, men such as Homer, Michelangelo and Shakespeare, owe to the beauty of their surroundings? All forms of art tend to reflect the spirit and conditions of their age. The fact that many of our modern art galleries and libraries are filled to overflowing with dull and listless works of art is a devastating reflection on our modern form of paganism. Men have ceased to believe in themselves or in the beauty of the world that surrounds them, and so they end up by not believing in the Creator of this world of beauty. It is a compliment to the spirit of faith of former ages that we can still visit places such as Stratford-on-Avon and Oxford and find therein rich peace and beauty.

The view of Stratford Grammar School, with its old guild chapel and half-timbered buildings, is well known as a classic picture postcard, but the reality is even more lovely.

In trying to trace back the various factors that may have influenced me in the growth of my vocation to the priesthood, it is not easy to identify any one thing in particular. Parents, relatives, friends, my love for my school, the loss of the family business, all these played their part, but high on the list must be the strong influence towards goodness that I learned from my headmaster, the Reverend A. C. Knight. He was typical of all that was best in the English form of holiness, being gentle, quiet and shy, and he had a calm dignity and mellowness of character that hinted at the depths of a rich and varied spirituality. God's ways are not our ways, and on the surface it may seem strange that a Protestant clergyman should have so influenced me towards becoming a Catholic priest. But one should remember that goodness is a universal thing, not the exclusive property of one class or creed.

Stratford Grammar School was a mixture of what is best in the public school system and the modern type of grammar school, and as things worked out in practice, I think we had the best of both worlds, half the boys being boarders and half day boys. The school claims to be one of the oldest in England and is rich in tradition, yet being a day-school it avoided the danger of becoming too divorced from real life and the vital influences of home.

The school buildings were a mixture of the old and the new. Most of us preferred the old part of the school and felt it was more conducive to study, in spite of the fact that by all modern planning laws these buildings were hopelessly out of date and inadequate and should long since have been condemned. The desks were centuries old and their surface was rough with the countless initials carved by schoolboys through the ages. Heating was by coal fires in huge dog-grate fireplaces. The windows were long and narrow. In practice, however, these rooms were warm and cosy in the winter and delightfully cool in the summer, whereas the new classrooms, like most modern classrooms with all their glass, were cold in the winter and like hothouses in the summer.

The teachers were learned and cultured men and most of them were completely dedicated to teaching and the welfare of their pupils. We were encouraged to develop our individual talents and to learn out of interest rather than out of fear and, as a result, there was a mutual respect between master and pupil. Discipline depended on a code of honour rather than on corporal punishment, and there were no abuses in the prefect system. In many ways our system of education was ahead of its time, maybe because it had its roots in the wealth of the past.

Forty years after I had left the school I one day took an American teacher to visit it. Imagine my surprise when the school porter told me that my old physics master, Mr Dyson, was still teaching there. As soon as he saw me he said: 'I remember you. You are Ingram and you won the slow bicycle race.' We entered his laboratory and, on the surface of things, it looked like a Heath Robinson nightmare, most of the equipment having been made by himself and the boys. My American friend looked down condescendingly at the wizened figure, but Mr Dyson had a twinkle in his eye when he said that he would show us his equipment. He pressed a button and immediately all the windows closed and the blinds shot down into position. Then he went on to demonstrate some of the intricate, self-made equipment and ended up by showing us the first-class observatory that he had built with the help of the boys. The revolving telescope was powered by a tiny electric motor that an old boy had found in the Kiel Canal during the fighting in the last world war. Mr Dyson so calculated it that it made exactly one revolution every twenty-four hours. He showed us excellent photos of the stars taken and printed by the boys. Modern educationalists speak of self-help and self-discovery among pupils as though this were a new thing in the field of education. They forget that these methods were being used by such men as Mr Dyson at least a generation ago.

One of the high spots of our school year was the football match which took place during the dinner break between the 'train' boys and the 'bus' boys. We played with a soft ball in the school playground and used the surrounding walls and buildings much as one uses the side cushions of a billiard table. The skill of the game consisted in being able to deflect the ball past one's opponent and against the nearest wall. As the boarders and town boys returned from dinner we often ended up with a hundred boys on each side and in this form the game returned to the basic origins of football. In some ways, however, it was a mixture of Rugby fives and the Eton wall game but without the latter's mud.

The late twenties were difficult times for Stratford-on-

Avon. Two things combined to save it from becoming too industrialized; these were the American tourists and the Flower brewery family. Few people could afford to run a car merely for pleasure and Stratford had not yet become a natural centre for motorists, neither were English people in those days very much interested in the birthplace of Shakespeare. It took the enthusiasm of the Americans to wake us up to the richness of our inheritance.

The old theatre was too small and inadequate and its company, in consequence, was mediocre. I remember how some of our school staff rejoiced when it was burned down, for this gave Stratford a chance to build a modern theatre more worthy of Shakespeare, and thus encourage a first-class company of actors to play there. The new theatre, designed by Miss Scott, was to be built in stone, but this was changed to brick because of the expense. When the theatre was completed, the locals christened it 'the Jam Factory'. Since then it has mellowed and now it blends happily into the soft landscape of the Avon banks. Much of the credit for this building must go to the Flower family and to the help which they received from America. Had this help not been forthcoming, Stratford might have been ruined for posterity.

The town had two festivals each year. In spring there were the celebrations in honour of Shakespeare's birthday, when the wide Bridge Street was decorated with the flags of many nations and the town paid homage to the man who was the chief source of their tourist trade. But, apart from Sam Bennett and his group of morris-dancers, there was little in these formal celebrations to attract a schoolboy.

The Mop Fair, which was held in autumn, was anything but formal. Town folk and country people met and combined to make it the great holiday of the year. Country people did not get official holidays in those days, apart from bank holidays, so the local fairs were the only free days they had. Traces of these fairs still survive in various parts of the country, but are now only dim shadows of their former glory.

Originally the fairs combined business with pleasure, for this was the time of the year when horses and cattle were sold or exchanged before winter began. Old men told me that they remembered seeing lines of farm-hands and dairymaids standing waiting to be hired for the next twelve months, all wearing the insignia of their craft. The maidservants held mops and thus gave the name to the fair.

Sometimes I played truant in order to join in the fun of the fair, and what a fairyland of excitement it was, especially at night when all the coloured lights of the stalls and sideshows were lit up in a blaze of glory. It was a schoolboy's paradise, and here I could see characters from the pages of Shakespeare, Chaucer and Dickens, laughing, talking, dancing, buying and selling, and enjoying themselves to the full. A huge ox was roasted in the main street and sandwiches made from it were sold in aid of the local hospital. It is not difficult to imagine Will Shakespeare strolling around in such a crowd and gathering a rich harvest of characters for one of his plays.

Chapter 4

TENSIONS AND DOUBTS

ADOLESCENCE marks a time of crisis that is spiritual as well as physical, for both soul and body undergo transformations and rapid growth. My adolescence was turbulent; everything seemed to be black or white, for I had not yet learned to appreciate the finer shades of life and love. At one moment I was the hero who pushes aside mountains as easily as molehills, but at the next I was plunged into an abyss of uncertainty and insecurity. In spite of these tensions, it was a fruitful time of deep and intense spiritual awakening. Hitherto I had accepted the explanation of life offered me on the authority of my parents and teachers, now I was forced to think things out for myself.

When I was about sixteen a trivial incident occurred which helped to pinpoint my thoughts on the basic realities of existence. I had borrowed a shotgun from some friends and gone hunting for rabbits in the bushes along the old tramway lines. My heart was racing with excitement as I stalked my prey. A rabbit came bounding out of the bushes into a clearing just ahead and sat up and looked at me, its ears twitching with curiosity. I pulled the trigger and it leapt into the air and then lay still. The suddenness of the change from bounding life to the awful quietness of death shocked me.

What was life and what was death? Did everything end at death? Was religion merely wishful thinking and a refusal of the human spirit to accept the possibility of annihilation? I felt cruelly torn between the comforting security of my Catholic faith with its firm belief in eternal existence and the fear that this might be only a dream.

For months I anxiously debated the question. Uncertainties and doubts in regard to such basic truths are hellhounds that torture the soul and destroy any real peace of mind.

This purgatory of mental agony lasted in my case for over a year. Afterwards I saw that it was a necessary experience for it meant that I could help in a practical way others who were undergoing similar experiences. Each one of us has to learn the hard way to come to grips with the fundamental problems of life and death. Granted that there is much that we will never fully understand, it is nevertheless essential for a full and happy life on this earth that one should know with certainty whether we continue our existence after our death or not, for the consequences profoundly affect everything that we do, and according to the manner in which we answer this question, so shall we pattern our lives.

It seems to me that there are roughly three ways of meeting this problem. First there is the Christian answer which insists on the existence of eternal life based on a depth-analysis of man, as man, and on God's revelation to man. Then there is the extreme view of a minority that there can be no life after death and that we are, at best, a superior type of animal, and nothing more than animals. Between these two beliefs are the views of those who are content to say that they are uncertain of the truth but are ready to treat God as a sort of spiritual insurance policy. Such an insurance policy demands only a very small premium of one's total energies. As long as one keeps the payments up to date, all will be well at the end!

I could not stomach an attitude of mind that uses God

as a spiritual umbrella whereby we can ignore him for most of our lives and then expect him to receive us with open arms when we come to its end. Christ has some very harsh words to say about those who are lukewarm in this life.

Like many other people, I was tempted to try to get rid of such thoughts by losing myself in activities. Fortunately, from force of circumstances, I was not able to dodge the issue in this way. During the summer months when grass was scarce it was common practice to graze one's cows along the wide roadside verges, and I had often to spend tedious hours in minding our cows in this way.

Most of my free time I spent in reading, but inevitably there would come a moment when I got tired and was forced to think. Not far from my home are the lovely old ruins of Hailes Abbey where one can find the charming Cistercian motto which sings the praises of solitude. It would seem that there are times in life when solitude is absolutely necessary if one is to come to terms with oneself and with God. Perhaps it is interesting that many of the spiritual leaders of mankind were shepherds? Moreover, it is a significant fact that men such as Moses, David and Patrick, St Paul and St Ignatius, after the first impact of their conversion, spent a period of solitude before starting out on their busy lives of preaching and organizing.

Boredom forced me to deepen my vision of reality, to cease seeking for it in an ever-widening world of external excitements, and to try to penetrate ever more deeply into the secrets of my own soul and of existence. To see self as self really is, without the props of activities, can be a shocking experience. But the advice of the ancient Greeks that man should get to know himself is as valid today as it ever was. It was a humiliating and purifying experience to have to face up to my limitations and shortcomings. There was an immense gap between my adolescent ideals and their realization. And yet I felt that man has a spark of divinity within him with which he can change his dream into reality if he truly wishes to do so.

Adolescence was for me a difficult time of divided loyalties, one half of myself clinging to boyhood, while the other was trying to face up to the responsibilities of manhood. For most of the time I was afraid. How many of us are afraid of our own fears? How many acts of violence and wars are due to fear?

About this time something happened that taught me not to be ashamed of fear, but to face up to it and learn to live with it. I loved all animals, especially dogs, but the animal that completely captured my heart was the donkey. There was something about a donkey that I found irresistible. We were finding the cycle ride and the long walk up the steep hill to mass every Sunday quite a grind, and it seemed silly to cycle when we had a fat pony at home. She was a lovely dappled grey called Jane, and she was the fastest pony in the district. The trouble was that I was too scared to drive her, for she had a nasty habit of bucking like a prancing bronco and bolting every time that she started on a journey.

One day we saw an advertisement for a donkey and trap for sale at Alcester and we decided to buy it, thinking that it would be easier for me to manage than our pony and that we could then drive to mass on Sundays. It took me fifteen hours to bring it the fifteen-mile journey home, for the donkey kept refusing to move and had to be dragged most of the way. How I longed for our pony and I then and there vowed never again to be afraid of her. The next day we resold the donkey and I drove Jane for the first time. It took me some time to learn the secret of dealing with headstrong ponies, which later on I was to find useful in dealing with headstrong people. Instead of pulling at the reins in fright as she pranced and danced, I let her gallop at full speed for several miles then, as she got out of breath and we came to a small hill, I flicked the reins and forced her on. One could feel her sense of amazement conveying itself along the length of the reins as she shook her head in surprise and galloped on again at full speed, and after this there was peace and understanding between us. It was not so much that I had mastered her, for she was far too proud to be mastered by any man, it was rather that we had come to terms of mutual respect, and after that I could do anything with her and she would obey instantly.

The country was now stagnant in the insidious grip of a terrible slump. Millions were out of work and there were few opportunities for young people unless they had money or influence to back them up. Farming was at a low ebb and one had to put in long hours of hard work for meagre results.

Seeing so many innocent people suffer forced me to think of the problem of evil and suffering and particularly to ask myself why a good God should permit the innocent to suffer. Seeking for an answer, I read everything I could lay my hands on and it seemed that, apart from the challenge of the Cross, no other answer made sense. The Christian message was certainly full of hope and love, but was it self-delusion to accept it, a despairing effort to come to terms with pain and suffering? Were Christians living in a world of pious make-believe and were they too afraid to face up to the bitter realities of life? Religion seemed to have all the answers, but was religion itself based on objective reality?

Apart from my early schooldays, I had received little formal religious instruction. As I attended a non-Catholic school, it had been arranged that my parish priest should give me private tuition once a week. Most of the time, however, we chatted about anything except religion. The priest suffered from ill health and was very lonely and frustrated in this small country parish and he often unburdened himself to me. At least this taught me the value of being a patient listener, but it did little to meet my spiritual doubts. I tried to tell him about them in general terms and he replied that he had been through a similar crisis when he was in his teens but that it had been resolved when he studied philosophy. After this he lent me a book on philosophy which I doubt if he had ever read. It was written by an idealist who was at great pains to try and prove that we did not exist except in a world of ideas. This was cold comfort to me, for it was bad enough to have doubts about the existence of God without having to doubt my own existence as well.

The human heart is made for certainty and when it lacks certainty it feels frustrated and very lonely. But I knew that it would be wrong to invent some man-made religion to exorcize my uncertainty. Religion, to be real, must come from God, not from man.

Most people have, of necessity, to go through some sort of a crisis of faith. Newman would explain it as the transition from a notional assent based on theory to a real assent based on experience. Between these two stages there inevitably lies a painful no-man's-land of doubt.

The transition from doubt to faith in God marks a genuine conversion of the soul. Much is written and taken for granted about the process of conversion, but we do not understand a great deal about it. There was little that was dramatic externally in my final conversion to faith in the existence of God.

Normally, the Holy Spirit works very slowly and almost imperceptibly in the soul until some small thing serves to achieve the final breakthrough. All too easily we can make the mistake of thinking that this particular thing is in itself the real cause of our conversion, forgetting that there have been a thousand small things that have been working in our soul over a long period of years to lead us to this end.

There are those who think that the various conversions of the soul towards God follow definite and exact stages of growth, somewhat similar to the stages of growth and crisis in the physical development of the body, such as the crises of puberty, adolescence and youth's transition into manhood. There may be some truth in this, though I suspect that there are many conversions going on all the time in the life of grace, and some of them, for various external reasons, appear to be more dramatic than others. For instance, it is true that St Paul's conversion on the road to Damascus seems to have been highly dramatic, but may it not also be true that there were probably many other conversions towards God in his soul, both before and after this one?

Some people, such as Professor Joad, come to believe in the existence of God because of the existence of evil in the world. As the years pass by, they come to realize that if there was no after-life then this world with its injustices and inequalities would be too terrible to contemplate.

My approach to God was the opposite of this. Gradually I came to believe in God because of my belief in the goodness of man. The overwhelming force that finally drove me to my knees was that of love, not of fear. Do not too many of us take this wonderful quality of selfless love too much for granted? Why should it exist in such abundance in the heart of man unless it reaches out beyond the sad limitations of finite time?

It was this ideal of goodness, manifesting itself in selfless loving, that gave me something worth while to cling to and formed the first all-important stepping-stone towards my belief in the existence of God. There were many people in my life whom I had loved, and the majority of them were good people. Most of these people were not Catholics and their views on religion differed sharply from my own, but their practice of goodness built up a strong bond of understanding between us.

But what finally convinced me of the existence of God was a small thing in itself. All my life I had had constant experience of the many anxieties and sacrifices my mother had to make in order to keep our home together and to pay our way. She had worked non-stop in the never-ending struggle to make ends meet, but the thing that impressed me most was the fact that she always seemed to have time and energy left over to help those in greater need than herself. If any of the poorer village women were taken ill she would be there within minutes to nurse them and take care of the children. I acted as the carrier of hot meals to these sick women and we kept a special basket wrapped in blanketing for this purpose. It was these small acts of kindness done by my mother which finally convinced me of the existence of God. Since then I have often wondered whether the thing that won people over to Christ was not so much his power of working miracles as the kind way in which he performed them. One thinks of the tremendous impact on our modern world made by good Pope John, but was not the real secret of his influence his overwhelming kindness? Yet without the existence of an all-loving God, kindness is a meaningless thing.

Chapter 5

THE BREAKTHROUGH

BEING by now convinced that God existed, the next thing for me to do was to study the claims of the Catholic Church. Was she founded directly by Christ, and were all other Christian Churches off-shoots from this parent stem? Was Christ God or was he only a holy prophet? Was the Bishop of Rome correct in claiming to be the descendant of St Peter? Questions such as these began to seethe through my mind.

From my practical experience of being brought up in the Catholic Church, there were many things about her that I loved, provided that her claims were valid. She was a religion of love, and even if her members, such as myself, often fell short of her high ideals, nevertheless those ideals were there before our eyes, challenging us. I loved the fearless way in which she defended truth at all costs and stood fast on principles, yet I also knew that in dealing with souls she was a merciful and tolerant Church according to the gentle spirit of Christ.

There were things of secondary importance that I did not like about the Church of my youth. It was tragic that the Catholic Church in England had lost its link with the vitality of artistic genius that had given such rich treasures in pre-Reformation times. Living in the Cotswolds, surrounded by many old wool churches built in Cotswold stone, I had developed a very critical standard regarding church architecture and furnishing. I loathed the many cheap imported plaster statues that were then to be found in our Catholic churches, and I disliked the stiff and over-decorated vestments. The way in which some priests gabbled through the Latin Mass, or the recitation of the Rosary, was also very annoying and it seemed silly to me to be praying to God in Latin when it was no longer a living language.

I decided to study the claims of the Catholic Church with an open mind. She must stand or fall by the analysis of objective truth and historical fact. Emotion, though it was there in the background, must not enter into the testing of her claims.

There was not then the spate of books about religion that there is today and the selection open to me was limited. Father Robert Eaton, of the Birmingham Oratory, an old friend of my family, sent us some of his works on the Scriptures and I read them, but found them rather dry. Newman was heavy reading and Belloc seemed obscure, though G. K. Chesterton was fascinating. Like my mother, I was an avid reader and had read most of the English classics by the time I was sixteen, and although these did not teach me much directly about religion, they taught me a lot about the potentialities for good and evil that are to be found in human nature.

One winter evening I went along our bookshelves to search out some old favourite. As my eyes ran over the shelves I caught sight of our family Bible and my memory went back to my early childhood when old Joe Veal had read out a passage to me. The memory of his love and reverence for the sacred text flooded back into my mind and I realized that herein lay the answer to my seeking. Within my grasp was the vital source of theology, so this should be my textbook and my guide. Acting on the impulse of the moment, I made up my mind to read through the Bible from cover to cover, no matter how long it might take me to do so. If the Catholic Church did not fit into this context I would have none of her.

I opened the Bible at the first page of Genesis and began to read carefully and thoughtfully. My reading continued all through the long winter evenings and, as time went by, I became more and more interested. Of course, there were the long, dull passages that one finds in most of the classics, but secular reading had prepared me for this.

It is not easy to explain the hold that the text had on me at that time. It seemed to absorb my whole being much as attendance at a university and making contacts with other minds might have done. I was soon to discover that the Bible is not so much a book as a whole library of books, written by different people over a period of centuries. Imagine a single volume containing works by Bede, Chaucer, Shakespeare and Dickens, and the idea helps one to understand the differences of mentality and style in the various authors of the Bible.

Some of the books are gems of literature while others are mediocre in literary quality. It is an over-simplification to judge the whole Bible as though it were one book.

Like many people I had retained the nursery idea that God was an old man with a long beard. Reading carefully through the Old Testament I realized how childish this was. The vital and living presence of God stood out on every page as being a Supreme Being of might and majesty, and yet at the same time a God of exquisite tenderness and compassion, with a patient and sympathetic understanding of man's weaknesses and mistakes.

Here was a history, not so much of mankind, but rather of the chosen people of God. It was also a deep and penetrating study of man himself and of his relationship with God. I saw in it a mirror of myself, my weaknesses and strengths, my doubts and certitudes, my hopes and fears. This almighty Father, towering above the chosen people, with all their virtue and fickleness, seemed to dominate me and give a sense of purpose and meaning to my life.

It was interesting to discover how many of the ideas that give richness to our classics have their roots in the Old Testament and to realize that the Hebrew mind is a deeply religious one, full of poetry and passion which depicts life in the dramatic contrast of primitive black and white. This strength of contrast matched my adolescent need. The Old Testament reminded me of the massive strength of Norman architecture with its simplicity of decoration and its effective use of the vivid contrast between light and shade.

Reading through the Bible as I did, concentrating on the text alone, refusing to be cluttered up by the long footnotes of the exegete, was an invaluable preparation for my future studies. If a priest does not do this there is a danger that he will get so entangled in the footnotes and explanations that he will fail to see the text as a composite whole and as a distinct entity. It might be a good thing if all novices had to spend the year of their novitiate in reading through the whole of the Bible.

The great characters of the Old Testament fascinated me – men such as Moses and David, women such as Judith and Esther. David was my favourite for in him I recognized a fellow-countryman and I linked his experience in tending sheep with my own in minding our cows by the roadside. He stood out in my mind as a mystic and a poet and yet as a man of action; a man who was as wise as an owl and as simple as a dove.

The poetic beauty of the Psalms appealed to me immensely and I used to read through some of them every day. Even though the original form of the poet's genius is partly obscured by the translation, the loveliness of these poems of praise still stands out. They are so disarmingly simple that they are impervious to the ravages of time. Throughout the centuries of Christianity they have been chanted daily by priests and nuns, and they never seem to grow stale through this constant repetition. No poet has yet succeeded in creating any other form of poetic art to replace them as the daily prayer of the Church.

Later on I came to understand that the secret of Hebrew poetry lies in its skilful use of a balanced harmony of thought and a subtle use of contrast and repetition of an idea. Mere repetition for the sake of repetition is dull and lifeless. The Hebrew poets had the rare gift of being able to take a simple idea and then contrast it with another idea which was partly the same and partly different. Their artistic genius consisted in the clever way in which they could take two apparently similar ideas and then highlight them by their subtle differences.

Many of our Lord's sayings are Hebrew poetry. For instance, in speaking of the lilies of the field he does not confine himself to comparing them with the glories of Solomon; he also contrasts them with the labour done by men and the spinning done by women, thus completing the balance of thought that was implied in the original idea. Passages such as the Lord's Prayer and the Magnificat are models of Hebrew poetry at its best.

It is most probable that David was inspired by the simple folk-songs of his day and he, in turn, inspired others who patterned their holy songs on his poetry. The background of the Psalms is largely that of country life, and unless one is in tune with this, one misses much of their beauty. The same holds good for much of the Gospel story.

But, if the countryside forms the background of the Psalms and of Hebrew poetry, in the foreground is man, with all his joys and sorrows, hopes and anxieties, failures and successes. What impressed me at that time was the constant struggle between anxious doubts and trusting faith that is so poetically portrayed in these songs of praise; they matched my own doubts and fears and gave me a promise of faith and hope.

One of the marks of any works of genius is that we get an insight into our own problems reflected in the mind of the author, and this deeper vision of reality helps us to penetrate into the depths of our soul.

My readings from the Scriptures showed me the sort of person that I was, someone full of contrasts, one moment bubbling over with hope, the next filled with doubt and fear; sometimes generous, more often selfish. Man is a complex bundle and I was a man, no better and no worse than any other. It seemed to me that the pattern of my life lay entirely in my own hands and that now I must be honest enough to face up to my weaknesses and avoid the temptation of blaming others for my failures.

It took me nearly a year to read the whole of the sacred Scriptures, and when I had finished I was so thrilled that I started reading them for the second time.

It was in this reading that I found my faith in God and in the validity of the claims of the Catholic Church; it also sowed the seeds of my vocation to the priesthood. The various books of the Bible were as coloured threads which did not make sense until the tapestry was seen as a whole. I soon forgot much of the detail, but the total vision of God's revelation to man was overwhelming in its truth and beauty. Everything seemed to slip into place. All sorts of small details, which at first sight appeared unimportant in themselves, built up into a composite picture of the coming of the Saviour of the world.

Where the Old Testament ended, the New Testament followed on as the triumphant entry of God into the personal affairs of man. Christ's birth, life, murder and resurrection made sense, not only of the Scriptures but also of my own existence. I had been forced to come to terms with sorrow, but here I could see how sorrow is counterbalanced by goodness and kindness. Although the existence of evil in a world created by an all-powerful God was still a mystery, I was now able to see how God could make use of this factor as a testing of man's free will in bringing about a greater good.

The Scriptures had a sense of timelessness and eternity. Men were born and died, cultures rose and fell, but the Word of God lived on for ever and was always alive and fresh to each generation. The words of Christ about bringing life more abundantly to this world were, I now realized, literally true.

For the first time for several years I felt my feet firmly secure on the rock of truth, and I knew that no matter what problems, doubts or anxieties I might have to face in the future, this refuge of security would always sustain me. I experienced a deep inner peace and contentment. There was little that was emotional about this feeling for it went much deeper than the emotions and seemed to penetrate my whole being.

It was exciting to rediscover the beauty and truth of the

Catholic Church at a much deeper level than ever before. Once I realized that the Catholic Church claims to be the life of Christ living on in the world, it then seemed the only logical answer to the fulfilment of the Scriptures. Without this living and vital reality of the life of Christ in the world of today the Scriptures would remain no more than an abstract and unrealized ideal; in truth, they form a bridge-head between early man and modern man, and it is a mistake to think of them as relating merely to the past, for Christ was not only an historical figure, he is also the dynamic source of our actual existence and living.

Certainly the Scriptures are the only link that can unite today's sadly divided Christians. It is interesting to note that it was a Scripture scholar, Cardinal Bea, for years the principal of the Biblical Institute in Rome, who was the man destined to pioneer the great ecumenical movement. He was one of the greatest figures in the Church of our century and in some ways he was to the Church of today what Newman was to the Church of the last century. Having been the confessor and spiritual director of Pope Pius XII, Cardinal Bea became the guiding force and inspiration behind Pope John and his Vatican Council.

As a child I had always experienced a strong sense of the Real Presence, and my union with Christ in the Eucharist was almost tangible, but now, after this rediscovery of my faith, I sensed the vital presence of Christ, not only in the Eucharist but also in all the good and lovely things and people of this earth.

This was not an emotional experience, but an intense inner awareness of reality. It is not easy to describe it in words for it has to be experienced to be understood. I felt the presence of something far greater than myself, like a sudden vision of eternity, and my anxieties and worries seemed so petty and insignificant by comparison with this everlasting reality. I was passionately fond of the English poets, but their awareness of beauty was only a dim shadow of my newly found awareness of Christ in all created things and in my fellow-men.

I felt an intense longing to attend daily mass and to receive Communion daily. I excluded from my mind the thought of becoming a priest for I had a high ideal of the priesthood and could not imagine myself being worthy of this vocation. I had yet to learn that God chooses men to serve him as priests, not because they are better than other men, but because he wants these men as his servants.

Flowing from my rediscovery of my Catholic faith, and my growing awareness of the vital presence of Christ in everything and everybody, was a greater consciousness of my many shortcomings and limitations. There was nothing morbid about this; it was the simple truth.

Meanwhile, besides my search for truth, I needed to plan my immediate life. The years of the depression had a stultifying effect on everybody; with millions out of work there were few opportunities for young people. The National Farmers' Union opened up the headquarters of their insurance company in a building opposite our school and several of my contemporaries joined their staff. For a time I was tempted to do the same as office hours would have made it possible for me to go to daily mass, but it seemed silly to choose a job that I did not like in order to be free to attend daily mass.

However, since the idea of attendance at daily mass had begun to dominate my life, I started to think of other ways which would make this possible. In the past I had often resented the long hours spent in helping out on our small farm, but by now I had grown to love farming and country life. Unfortunately, I also knew that a farmer's day started much too early to allow for going to daily mass.

Chapter 6

A WORKSHOP, A VOCATION AND AN INSURANCE OFFICE

WHEN the time came for me to leave school, my future was still undecided. The only way by which I would be able to go to daily mass would be to have my own business, and for a time I toyed with the idea of trying to restart my father's business, developing the gate and ladder side of it, but there seemed no future to it.

Then a friend of ours who worked at the General Electric Company at Birmingham suggested my becoming an apprentice there and studying for a degree in electrical engineering. My elder sister was teaching in Birmingham which meant that I would be able to stay with her. She lived in the Oratory parish in Edgbaston and the G.E.C. factory was situated on the other side of the city at Whitton. The journey from my room to my work was several miles. Sometimes I cycled and at others got a lift in the car of a fellow-apprentice. He had a supercharged Austin Seven. Not many of these cars were made, but they had a performance as good as the Mini Cooper. In those days there was little traffic and by taking several short-cuts down side streets he made the journey in about eleven minutes. Another apprentice friend had an air-cooled three-wheeler Morgan which could do 103 miles an hour, but it was tricky on corners. In the twenties motoring was still an adventure and there was a tremendous feeling of chivalry among motorists. Breakdowns were frequent and most drivers, out of necessity, were good mechanics and would always stop to help another motorist in trouble.

This drive across a city was in dramatic contrast to my country journeys. It came as a shock to me to realize my good fortune in having always been surrounded by beauty, fresh air and clear Cotswold skies. Parts of Birmingham were quite pleasant and the people were warm-hearted and friendly, but some of the areas through which we passed were terribly drab and dirty. The depression was at its worst and each day we saw groups of half-starved men hanging round the street corners. It was terrible to see the dull, listless look in their eyes. The dole was better than nothing in that it kept people alive, but it was a shocking form of existence, both soul-destroying and degrading.

Although I had had to work very hard on our small farm, and had known what it was to go short of luxuries, I had not the slightest idea of the degradation of abject poverty. The ugliness and drabness of the slums was made all the more tragic because of their contrast with the palatial buildings and the shops crammed full with every type of goods that stood in the city centre.

As a farmer I was used to the mud and slush of cattle gateways and the muck of the farmyard in autumn rains, and I had known what it was to have my hands caked with earth, but this was a clean sort of dirt compared with the clinging and penetrating grime of the city slum or the factory floor, and, besides this, the smoke-polluted atmosphere blotted out the sun and discoloured the buildings.

Later I discovered that there were clean and happy homes in the midst of these slums, but that is no excuse for the conditions which make slums inevitable. The fact that human nature has the spirit within it to rise above such horrors can never justify us in allowing such conditions to exist and my blood used to boil as I travelled through these slums. I was as ashamed and involved as when the fox-hounds were tearing that badger to pieces, and I felt the need to try to do something to help to do away with the social injustices that we had inherited from the last century and to prevent them from being taken for granted. My helplessness in not being able to do much about it only increased my frustration.

The second shock that hit me was my experience of the soul-destroying monotony of factory life. The G.E.C. factory was one of the finest in Europe and working conditions were very good, but to me it seemed like a prison. The shops had row upon row of noisy machines with hundreds of youths, men and women bending over them in adoration, as though they were acolytes of the machine god. Plenty of jobs on our farm were monotonous, but one was dealing with living things and there was a sense of purpose in all that one did.

The noise in some of the machine-shops was an inferno. Ordinary conversation was impossible and one had to stand within a few inches of a person and shout instructions to be heard above the din. In part, out of grim necessity, one got used to this incessant noise, but it had a blunting and dulling effect on the senses.

In one of the machine-shops there were rows of drilling-machines manned by boys of fourteen who had just left school. Many were undernourished and all had sallow complexions and I noticed that their skins glistened like the old-fashioned tallow candles that hung from the rafters in our village shop. The sight of these boys moved me profoundly and I felt a restless urge to do something to help to abolish the poverty of their living conditions.

After I had been there for six months I was called to the general manager and he told me that the time had now come for me to sign the apprenticeship contract which would bind me for six years, and that during this period I would have to attend night classes and study for a degree. This man had some eight thousand workers under him and, like most people who are real leaders, he was simple in manner and very friendly. He asked me if I was happy at my work and ready to sign my contract. I found it easy to confide in him so I told him how deeply I felt about the poverty that I saw around me and how much I wanted to do something about it. He was very kind and listened patiently, and then asked me what I thought I could do to help.

His question came as a challenge and suddenly everything came clear in my mind. Looking more deeply into the underlying causes of poverty, it seemed that it was not so much social conditions that caused poverty as the moral decisions that made bad social conditions inevitable. The root-causes of poverty were often those of selfishness and greed. One cannot force men to act with justice towards each other by Acts of Parliament, as the unscrupulous will always find ways and means of getting round man-made laws. In the deeper issues it is a question of morality, and men must be urged to act with justice towards each other of their own free will. The man most suited to do this urging was the dedicated priest, for such a man had nothing to gain, materially speaking, for himself.

These thoughts flashed through my mind while the manager was waiting for my answer. Much to my own surprise, I found myself saying that the best way for me to do something was by becoming a priest. The general manager nearly tumbled off his chair at this unexpected reply, but he was nothing like as astonished as I was myself. It is strange how the Holy Spirit works in the soul. Often one spends months or years seeking for a solution to a problem and then, when one least expects it, some small incident occurs which sparks off the answer in a blinding flash of light.

That same evening I went to see one of the priests at the Oratory. He was a man who was very much in tune with the gentle kindness of Cardinal Newman, for the spirit of Newman still broods over the Birmingham Oratory. He suggested that I talk things over with Father Lester, a Jesuit priest, who ran the training college for late vocations at Osterley.

Father Lester invited me down to Osterley for the weekend. He was the smallest Jesuit in the world, being only four feet two inches in height, but what he lacked in inches he made up for by the bigness of his heart. He had started Osterley as a training centre to help men returning from the 1914–18 war to complete their preparatory studies for the priesthood. It is still flourishing and over a thousand priests have now been helped there.

For some time we discussed the possibility of my having a vocation to the priesthood. Suddenly he paused and told me very definitely that he thought I should become a priest and join the Society of the Divine Saviour, which had its headquarters in Birmingham.

At that time I was completely ignorant about religious life and knew nothing of the various religious Orders. I had never heard of the modern types of religious Congregations and Societies or of their efforts to imitate the life of

Christ in as literal a manner as is possible in the contemporary world. Certainly the life of the enclosed monk held no attraction for me; what I wanted was to imitate Christ as directly as possible by being in the world and yet not of the world.

Father Lester insisted that I should take a small booklet about the Salvatorians, as the members of the Society of the Divine Saviour are called. I accepted it out of politeness, making a mental note that these people were quite the last that I would wish to join.

At school I had dropped Latin to do more science, and now it would be necessary for me to complete my Latin before beginning my higher studies for the priesthood. Father Lester arranged for me to enter Osterley House of Studies in the coming autumn.

Cycling home from the station I caught up with a local farmer's daughter. As we chatted I began to have my first doubts about my vocation and I wondered if I had not been too hasty and was perhaps more suited to married life.

Such doubts were to be typical of the next three years. At one time I was certain that I had a vocation; at another I was desperately uncertain. For the most part I fought against the idea and looked for excuses which would enable me to dodge the issue. There was certainly never any question of my being forced into the priesthood, rather I did everything to convince myself that I had not got a vocation.

Shortly after my return home my mother was taken very ill, and when the autumn term started at Osterley, I was unable to leave her. Secretly, this was a welcome excuse, as it gave me a valid reason for putting off my decision and, anyway, it seemed best to wait until I was twenty-one before committing myself. Having rushed into the idea of becoming a priest in a matter of seconds, the choice would have to stand or fall by the acid test of time.

I hated the idea of leaving my mother on her own after all the hard work and sacrifices she had made to ensure our schooling. My eldest sister was still teaching in Birmingham and my other sister was planning to go to London to start her training as a nurse, so at present I was needed at home.

Fortunately, my mother had, with her pension, a sufficient income on which to live, for if not I could never have contemplated leaving her. When her health improved my ambition turned to earning enough money to pay for my future studies and to do so I was prepared to take any job in which I could save enough money to achieve this purpose. In the end I got one in an insurance office at Witney, lodging there during the week and going home for the week-ends.

All my life I have been a keen motor-cyclist, for on a cycle one has a much closer contact with the countryside than in a car. I had bought my first motor-bike for ten shillings when I was sixteen. It was a 1904 model and was driven by a belt drive. It had no gears or clutch, and if it was necessary to halt in traffic one had to stop the engine; also, it had to be pushed to start and one had to jump on to the saddle while it was in motion. When I gave my sister a lift, she had to wait some fifty yards down the road and then, as I passed by, take a flying leap on to the pillion seat. Sometimes she missed and landed on the road, but this only added to the fun.

Now I bought a fast machine, and this was to be my passport to the discovery of the varied beauty of the Cotswolds. On my first journey to Witney, it was a shock to discover that the warm and friendly stone of the north

Cotswolds could change so quickly into the cold grey stone of Oxfordshire, and for the first time I realized that each county has its own character and individuality. It took me a long time to appreciate the beauty of Oxfordshire.

My journey took me through sleepy Shipston on Stour. This was the place where I had run away at the age of five to see our local football team play in the Cup-tie, and had returned home, footsore and tired out, to find the village policeman searching for me and my parents frantic with anxiety.

After some miles I climbed the steep hill at Long Compton and over the ridgeways near to the Cotswold Stonehenge of the Rollright Stones with its distant view of the Avon valley. I skirted Chipping Norton and passed close to Heythrop College, the centre of theological studies of the Jesuits in England. I saw some of the students out walking and their black clothes reminded me of my own possible vocation. Little did I then imagine that I would spend four years there doing theological studies, and would return years later to help start the expansion of the Heythrop project of central studies for priests, nuns and laity.

Now I passed through the charming old town of Charlbury which, with nearby Woodstock, was famous for its cottage industry of glove-making. The road then led me on to Burford with its steep main street and lovely old stone houses. At that time it had a bell foundry. From here to Witney the road was bleak and barren, although the view of the Windrush valley below was very lovely.

Witney stone seemed to us cold and grey, but my lodgings were warm-hearted and friendly. Mass was celebrated in a temporary hall and the parish priest, Father Lopes, travelled over from Eynsham. He was a convert clergyman and did tremendous work in this area.

When any of the insurance agents were ill I had to take over their rounds and thus got to know the Cotswolds very thoroughly and became very interested in their history as well as in the local crafts. Their beauty lies, not so much in their rolling hills, as in their lovely houses. The colour of the stone varies from dull grey to every shade of warm golden yellow. The charm of the old buildings is largely due to the courses of stone which are irregular and uneven and, because of this, have a variety of light and shade.

The gracious stone churches, some of which are as large as cathedrals, were built out of the fortunes made by the wool merchants in the Middle Ages. During these times, the constant wars in Europe meant that continental farmers could not rear sheep for wool as their flocks were killed for food by the soldiers; and it was because of this that the peaceful Cotswold hills became wealthy centres of the wool industry. Gloucestershire then had more churches and abbeys than any other county and was called 'God's County', and 'As sure as God is in Gloucestershire' was a well-known saying.

Cotswold farms are some of the most interesting in the world, for the older ones often form an entire village of their own, with cottages, inn, duckpond and village green clustered around the farm buildings. Some of them have elegant stone-built dovecotes which house hundreds of doves and thus provide a store of fresh meat when supplies are low. The fields are fenced in with dry stone walls, the flat stone being ideal for this purpose. These walls are built by tapering them inwards on a broad base. The open joints give a sense of texture and reflect the light and shade in intricate patterns.

The straddle stones on which the corn ricks used to be built to keep the corn clear of damp and rats are like gigantic toadstools.

Cotswold towns and villages are usually built in the shelter of the valleys, though Stow-on-the-Wold, where the Devil is reputed to have caught a cold, is the exception. The water-mills in the streams of these valleys provided the power for industry at the start of the Industrial Revolution and were used until the discovery of steam-power. Traces of this industry survive at places such as the tweed mills of Stroud and Chipping Norton and the blanket mills at Witney.

Part of the charm of the Cotswolds lies in the purity of its atmosphere and the splendour of its skies. Sometimes, after a storm, the clouds drift along the horizon like sheets billowing on a clothes line. The evening sun casts long shadows among the hills and clings to the stone buildings as though it were reluctant to go to bed.

While at Witney I managed to save about a third of my wages, but as I was in a hurry to have sufficient to pay for my studies by the time I was twenty-one, I left this job and invested my savings in a garage at Hereford, where I was to train as a salesman.

After some days the man who said he owned the garage disappeared with my money and that of several other men, some of whom were swindled out of their life's savings. Eventually he was caught by the police and it turned out that he was an ex-solicitor who had been struck off the rolls for dishonesty. This experience was a hard blow to both my pocket and my pride, though it taught me not to trust in myself but to cast all my cares on God. It also forced me to search into myself through prayer.

Chapter 7

A THRIVING BUSINESS AND AN INNER STRUGGLE

AFTER this humiliating failure I resolved to fling myself into farming and hoped that, even if times were difficult, it would be possible to make the money I needed by dint of hard work and effort. The years that followed were full of happiness and I came to love farming and country life. My brief taste of life in a city had made me thank God for the blessings of the countryside, and there was a part of me that was deeply stirred by this direct contact with nature.

I came to realize that each season has its special beauty and that, in some ways, winter has just as much charm as spring or autumn. The delicate tracery of the trees stands out to greater advantage in wintertime and then the Cotswold hills are purple back-cloths against the leaden skies.

I learned to follow nature's changing moods from hour to hour and discovered that there were a few seconds on most days when she was hushed and at peace and seemed to echo something of divinity. This close contact with nature developed all my senses; for instance, when my blood was tingling and my muscles taut with hard work, I was more responsive to the tang of the earth on my fingers and the different scents of plants and grasses in my nostrils, and, besides this, the slap of heavy rain on my cheeks, the frost on my toes and fingers, the burning of the midday sun, the scratching of stubble in harvest-time, the rustle of dead leaves in autumn, were challenges to an ever deeper communion with nature.

This demanded involvement from me; it came partly in the care of animals. It is a proven fact that animals thrive better when they can find close points of contact with their masters. They have many of the same qualities as children and can be just as demanding.

Caring for them was a twenty-four-hour job. Sheep broke out, cows calved, pigs had their litters, at the most inconvenient times of the day and night.

I was tied to my animals almost as a mother is to her children, yet it was good to be one's own master and to be able to take a break when in the mood for it. Most of my holidays were working holidays, taken to attend markets and auction sales. Visiting a cattle market seemed to me like taking a leap back into medieval England. In fact, its roots went much deeper than this, for in many ways it was like taking part in the kind of battle of wits that has excited mankind in every age and culture.

The auctioneer played a dominant role in our lives, for he held in his hands the thread of our fate and determined whether there would be sufficient money from the sale of our stock to pay for the rent only, or whether there would be a surplus for profit. I listened to his rapid patter with a thumping heart, and when he reached the stage when the price wavered between no profit and profit, the excitement was unbearable. His was no easy task, for he had to try and please both buyer and seller, and he could only do this by striving to be scrupulously fair. He sat enthroned above the auction ring like a High Court judge in session.

Farming, in all its varied forms, is one of the most highly skilled crafts that there is and it takes half a lifetime to learn all its finer points. We had to plan our crops years ahead and it needed much business acumen to be able to judge future markets and demands. One had to be resourceful too in the maintenance of farm machinery, for farm plant is expensive and varied; many of our machines were invented by farmers themselves.

Nowadays a lot of the skilled crafts have been replaced by the technical skills of machinery, but in those days small farmers had to do most tasks by hand. What a thrill it was when I built my first hayrick! It took me quite a time to acquire this skill, the secret being to keep the middle well filled, so that the rain would flow off the hay. After the rick had settled, we had to pull out the loose hay at the sides and tidy the rick into shape, the spare hay being used to top up the ridge of the roof. We used our best straw for thatching. This had to be raked out into clean and straight bundles which were fixed down securely with string and rick-pegs, the pegs being inserted at an angle so that the rain did not penetrate the roof. There was a tradition that all corn-ricks had to have a woven straw crown fixed on their ridges. We used to vie with each other to see who could build the neatest rick. Extra attention was given to what we called the London side, which was the side nearest to the road and public view.

When the corn had dried out, a man would travel round the countryside with his threshing-machine, which was powered by a huge steam-engine. Its owner idolized this engine and tended it with loving care and devotion. There is an attraction about a steam-engine that defies description and which is completely lacking in a petrol-engine. Steam locomotive enthusiasts come under this magic spell, but what it is, it is not easy to say. Maybe it is because a steam-engine seems to be a living thing and is responsive to the touch of its master, like the mighty charger of a medieval knight.

Ploughing with a team of horses may seem to an onlooker to be extremely boring for the ploughman who plods his way to and fro across a big field and covers some twenty miles a day. In point of fact, it is full of variety, and the plough cuts through the ground as though it were alive. Some of the old wooden ploughs which we then used had lovely flowing lines, rather like those of a sailing boat, and their design varied from county to county according to the nature of the local soil, clay soil, for instance, needing a different type of design to sandy soil.

When ploughing a large, flat field, the first thing we did was to mark the exact centre of the field with a straight line of twigs. The team of horses were then driven along this line by sighting the twigs between the horses' ears, much as a fighter pilot aligns his plane for an attack. Having started along this line, it was fatal to look back for a check-up. Hence the point of the Gospel story about not looking back.

These horse-drawn ploughs could only plough in one direction, and thus the soil would be pushed in the opposite direction on the return journey. This meant that it was pushed up towards the centre according to the width of the turn, and the whole field would be ploughed in a series of ridges and furrows. These had to coincide with the land drains underneath the furrows. When the ridges became too high, they were split down the centre by ploughing in the opposite direction. Ploughing by tractor has changed all this, as the tractor shares can be adjusted for a change of direction. This is why fields are now flat, rather than a series of ridges and furrows, and if today one sees a meadow with ridges and furrows it means that the last time it was ploughed it was done by horses.

When I was a boy there were still a few teams of oxen being used in the Cotswolds. Horses travel faster than oxen but they can only work an eight-hour day, whereas oxen can work for ten hours. To drive a team of four horses on a long rein, and to turn them and the plough at the end of the furrow, demanded skill. Sometimes the plough kicked as it cleaved its way through the hard soil, and it was fascinating to watch the furrow of earth twist and break as it was turned over by the shining shares. During the wet and cold weather the ploughman usually wore a corn-sack over his shoulders. By tradition, ploughmen always wore corduroy trousers and these were hitched up by a leather strap fastened under the knee. They carried a long whip, not to use on the horses but to crack like the shot of a pistol. Some farmers would deliberately choose small men as their carters, so that the team would look all the bigger in comparison. The horses were magnificent beasts, weighing nearly half a ton each; they were trained to obey the traditional horse language which varied from county to county and had been handed down through the generations.

An old ploughman once taught me the secret of lighting a fire on a windy, wet day without the aid of paper. He selected a few dead twigs from the hedgerow and then whittled them into fan-shaped shavings with his pen-knife and thus had tinder for starting the fire. A ploughman would sit by such a fire on a bitterly cold day and eat his cold lunch of bread and cheese, while his horses fed out of nosebags, their steaming flanks covered with corn-sacks.

Another skill we learned was hedge-laying, and there was great rivalry between us as to who could lay the neatest hedge. To do this, the hedge was allowed to grow up to ten feet or more. It was necessary to wear heavy leather gloves to handle the thorns. First, the rough stuff was cut out from the hedge, so that only the straightest branches were left standing. These were then half severed at the bottom and bent over on top of each other and twisted round stakes which had been cut out of the rough branches. Long lengths of the thinnest branches were twisted round the top of the stakes to keep the hedge in position. The secret of good hedge-laying was to be sure and press the growth well down to the bottom as this prevented sheep from making holes in the hedge afterwards. Sheep are very difficult to fence in, as they like to roam and find out the weak spot in any fence.

Scything was another country skill which took me quite a time to learn. Eventually I found that one had to keep the heel of the scythe firmly pressed on the ground while it was swung in a wide arch. It was also essential to keep it very sharp by using a whetstone. This was carried in a leather pouch fastened to one's belt.

Many of the country crafts, if carried out correctly, have a definite rhythm and pattern of movement that is rather like a stately dance. There comes a stage of perfection in most crafts when work is transformed into play and when hands and feet weave intricate and balanced patterns of motion that border on poetry.

As our farm was only a small one, and as we were short of grazing land for our cattle, we developed a herd of pedigree pigs. We worked on the mixed-farming principle whereby we produced most of our own feeding stuffs and, as far as was possible, each of our products was closely interrelated to the others. We did not sell our milk but made it into butter, using the skimmed milk for fattening our young pigs. Before we bought a machine to separate the cream from the milk we used to put the milk out into large shallow bowls in our cellar, and as the cream rose to the surface, it was skimmed off by hand with a scoop. We sold our butter at the grocery stores at Shipston on Stour and it commanded the top price. The secret of making good butter is to scald the cream before it is churned as this removes any possible taint that may have been picked up from the feeding stuffs.

I invented what was possibly one of the first pneumatic wheelbarrows. Had I realized its potential at that time, I might have made a fortune. It was made out of an old car-wheel, and though it looked clumsy and people laughed when they first saw it, they soon stopped laughing when they took in how effective it was over soft ground.

Farming is rather like sailing before the mast. Three-quarters of it is hell, but in the remaining quarter one comes near to heaven, and all the hard slog is forgotten. It is very like the joy one gets out of tending a garden; that is no doubt why most farm gardens are rather neglected, for a farmer has no need of a garden since his whole farm is one large garden.

No two of my days on the farm were ever alike, as there was such a variety of jobs to be done. No matter what our plans might have been the night before, a sudden change in the weather would demand a complete change of work. The uncertainty of the English climate meant that we had to be constantly on the alert in an effort to keep one step ahead of it. But I think that to live in a country where the weather is more settled would take half the fun out of farming. Nature is a stern and relentless adversary, but she is also the farmer's best friend if he is true to her laws.

One never knew when something completely unexpected would happen. It could be the sudden flash of a kingfisher on the wing, or the brilliance of a woodpecker, or sometimes on a dull and wet day the sun would come out for a few seconds and light up the wet bark of a dead tree with a shimmer of silver, or the moon would weave patterns in the November mist as it clung to the valleys and mantled the hills. Usually, these rare moments of beauty came when one least expected them, and if ever I set out to find them, they did not happen. Yet one had to be in a responsive mood to see things such as the rainbow of colours reflected in a cobweb on a frosty morning, or the glint of light reflected on the raven-black waters of a stagnant pool.

I went on with my daily readings of the Psalms and they made a deep impression on me and helped me to lift my mind from the beauty that is to be found in nature to the more lasting beauty that is to be found in the life of the spirit. Here was a deeper form of loveliness that stood impervious to the changing seasons and the passing of time. I realized that if my life was to have depth of purpose and meaning, it must be built on something more solid than Cotswold stones and changing seasons.

This growing awareness of the beauty of the life of the soul kept bringing my thoughts to the life of Christ and how his influence has enriched our daily lives. Religion is not some sort of best suit that is worn only on a Sunday. Rightly understood, it gives depth and meaning to all our days, and without it life is as empty and dreary as marriage without love.

There was little that was soft or sentimental in my feelings about religion. It was something that was forced upon my mind out of the logical consequences of my life and problems. Just as the relentless laws of nature forced me to be obedient to her service if our farm was to flourish, so was it necessary for me to be obedient to God's laws if my life was to be full and happy. Nature will not tolerate any cheating and neither will God.

In my early experience of dealing with animals as a youth, my first instinct had been to try to take short-cuts wherever possible, and it was only by making sad mistakes that I was forced to see that the hardest way to do any job is usually the quickest and best in the long run. It is exactly the same in the life of the spirit. Each of us has to learn the hard way. Eternity is far too important to be treated lightly.

One of the most valuable things that I learned during these years of farming was the essential need for treating animals with love and kindness. Later on in my life as a priest, I came to understand how important this is in dealing with people. An animal will respond willingly only to kindness, and with love and patience one can train it to do almost anything.

Perhaps the Holy Spirit was preparing me for my final break with farming, for it was a fact that everything I touched seemed to turn to gold. Things prospered in such a way that we were able to build up our stock ready for a successful sale. The livestock sold in country areas went for much lower prices than in the markets nearer to Birmingham, so I began to buy stock at these country markets and sell it at a good profit in the town markets.

Indeed, in spite of the depression, we were now doing so well at farming that this prosperity became a serious temptation to me to abandon the idea of becoming a priest. It seemed a risky thing to lose the certainty of making a good living out of farming against the uncertain chance of my having a genuine vocation to the priesthood. Furthermore, I had grown to love farming so much that I would have welcomed taking over a badly neglected larger farm in order to develop its full potential.

Some of my old school-friends were already married and, having experienced the happiness of caring for baby animals, I thought it would have been good to have had my own children to care for. While I fully believed that for a priest to be completely dedicated to a spiritual family it is best for him to remain single, I was worried about whether I was going to be strong enough to make this necessary sacrifice.

Most of our friends were not Catholics and they found it hard to understand why I should wish to leave the enticing opportunity that had opened out before me. One old business friend took me aside and gave me a lecture, telling me it was my duty to stay at home and make a lot of money for my mother. When I said I was not interested in making a lot of money he looked at me as though I was weak in the head.

But my growing love for farming, my thoughts of marriage, my anxiety for my mother, all these problems, though important in themselves, were secondary to my doubts about my vocation. I felt that if once I could be certain about that, then all my other problems would sort themselves out. This did not mean that I did not have a deep feeling for my mother; it was rather that if I became a priest, then one form of loving would be outweighed by another.

Some men know quite clearly from an early age that the priesthood is their calling: for them their choice may be relatively smooth in its first stages of growth. Where this is the case, they not infrequently meet their problems during the course of their studies. In my case, most of my doubts came before I started.

The Holy Spirit does not normally call men to the priesthood in a dramatic way, or by some external sign. The call is usually something that builds itself up out of many small events and circumstances. The passing of time is the real test.

A priest is just as human as any other man; in fact, he should be more human than most men if he is to fulfil his priestly job. But while he is not necessarily more holy than the average layman, it is essential that he should love goodness more than anything and have a strong urge to do good. It is this attitude of mind that is all-important because a priest must be striving towards an ideal, even if he never reaches its fulfilment.

During these years of inner struggle I often tried to convince myself that I had not got a vocation, but this urge came back again and again. I kept seeking for alibis without success and hoping against hope that something would happen to decide the issue in such a way that I would not have to make this sacrifice. Conscience is a strange and persistent thing. It refuses to be fobbed off with excuses. The more I struggled against this quiet but incessant demand, the stronger grew the urge within me. Often I was forced to seek some sign in prayer and all I found was uncertainty and doubt.

Chapter 8

MY DOUBTS VANISH

THE answer to my doubts came in quite an unexpected way. One evening I went over to Chipping Campden for Benediction. The parish priest was a warm-hearted, bluff north-countryman who was more at home with a cricket bat in his hands than with books. He had a terrible stammer but all the same insisted on preaching for half an hour as a matter of conscience.

That evening, in the middle of a rambling sermon, he suddenly stopped and, quite out of context, queried why he had become a priest. This jolted me for it seemed as though it were being addressed to me personally though this priest knew nothing of my problems. In my life as a priest I have had similar experiences. One says something quite out of context during a sermon or a retreat and thereby solves somebody's problem. Such incidents seem to be the working of the Holy Spirit.

This priest now told us that the driving force that had urged him on to the priesthood had been love. This simple statement made a deep and lasting impression on me, partly because of the way he said it, and partly because he was such a very shy and British-bulldog type of character that one did not expect him to speak out about love in this blunt way. As he said these words the mists cleared before my eyes and I saw in an instant that herein lay the secret of a priest's vocation.

Not only did I see this truth as an abstract principle, but the inner depths of my whole being grasped it as an intense and dynamic reality. Moments such as these are very rare. In them one suddenly sees the inner kernel of reality and life takes on a new dimension. Newman sums up this experience as being the difference between a notional assent that is based on theory and a real assent that is based on valid experience.

I was reminded of Christ's teaching when he speaks of the blindness of the Pharisees who had eyes but could not see. Until now I had been groping my way through shadows and stumbling from crisis to crisis. I had had a vague ideal connected with religion and Christ, and my hopes of becoming a priest were based on an equally vague ideal of service, but they lacked definition and the cohesion of dynamic purpose and inner drive. So must the apostles have felt when they first met Christ. They admired his ideals but did not feel personal commitment and involvement, and so they carried on with their fishing. All their lives they had been fishermen and they must have had dreams of landing a bumper catch. Christ won their hearts by giving them the catch of their lives, so big as to swamp their boats. It was at this moment that they saw the Christ-ideal for the first time in all its depth, and it is typical of the human heart that, having now had their material wishes fulfilled, they left this catch of fish behind and followed Christ as fishers of men.

During recent months I had been reading Newman and had been both fascinated and puzzled by his 'Lead, Kindly Light'. I found it difficult to understand why he asked not to see the distant scene and was satisfied with one step at a time. Now I understood that he was speaking of that insight whereby the soul sees so intensely into the depths of reality that there is, as yet, no room for the distant scene.

This deep and inner conversion of the soul towards God was not the sort of emotional experience that some of Wesley's followers seem to have experienced, though it is possible that what was lasting in those conversions was based on realities far deeper than the emotions. It is likely that the deeper conversion towards a greater awareness of spiritual realities which I now experienced had been slowly building itself up towards a breaking point over the past few years and this particular sermon had merely triggered off what was latent within.

It is not easy to know just how much such experiences owe to natural causes, or to the workings of supernatural grace; probably there is a subtle combination of both. The soul seeks for its creator and may spend years looking in the wrong places until quite unexpectedly it stumbles over some small truth that penetrates the mists of doubt like a flash of lightning. Francis Thompson, in his 'Hound of Heaven', describes his experiences in this search after truth. He sought for happiness in every kind of experience, until the Hound of Heaven tracked him down and, alone and at bay, he was forced to face up to God as the source of all happiness.

Because of his great love for man, God the Father sent his son into the world to save man, and Christ saved man through the fullness of his priesthood. This ideal of Christ the priest would be my ideal. It is a sad thing that any talk about goodness, or attempt to strive after goodness, should in our modern world so often be mistaken for mock piety. It is not only sad, but contrary to all the known facts. There is not a single person who does not know that goodness is the only thing that is of lasting value in our age, as in any other age. Goodness goes far too deeply into the soul of man to be faked. It flows from selfless love and is nourished on love, and it sums up all the finest qualities that we admire in others. The fact that some people may put on an outward show of goodness is no argument against the value of genuine goodness. Goodness survives when all else is long forgotten. It gives colour and depth to the beauty of existence and makes life well worth living. Without goodness, our world is empty and drab. Selfish people are the most boring of all, for they are so engrossed in themselves that the world is imprisoned in the narrowness of their outlook, whereas goodness opens up new worlds of hope and opportunity.

It is a pity that English people are so shy in talking about religion. Part of this shyness may be due to their innate respect for religion, but it would be better if they would discuss their feelings more openly. My long experience as a priest has proved to me that the majority of people have a deep hunger after goodness, and that this goodness is but another name for God.

To become a priest it is not sufficient to like and admire goodness; one has to love it with one's whole being. It has to be the driving force of one's whole life, overruling all things else. My limitations now struck me more forcibly than ever, but I consoled myself with the thought that no man is ever worthy of the priesthood, and one has to leave it to God's love to bridge the gap between ideal and fact.

After my experience at Chipping Campden I flung myself into farming with greater zest than ever before, my one aim being to make enough money to pay for my training. My mother sensed the change in me and suggested that I should go away to test out my vocation. The fact that the initiative came from her pleased me, for the thought of leaving her alone was a constant anxiety. Being very obstinate, I still wanted to be financially independent, but I wrote to Father

Lester, asking for his advice and telling him that it would take me a further five years before I had saved sufficient money to cover the cost of my training. He replied by return, saying that he would help me out of the Osterley Fund and that five years of the priesthood were far too precious to lose for lack of money.

He asked me to go and visit the Father Provincial of the Salvatorian Fathers who now had a house at Wylde Green, Birmingham, and attended lectures at Oscott College. I had often thumbed through the pamphlet which he had given me some years before and I was still not attracted by them. However, out of respect to Father Lester, I decided to visit them, though I felt convinced that I would never join them.

The front door of Wylde Green House was opened by a smiling novice who happened to be a young man who had visited our parish some years before, shortly after his conversion to the Catholic faith. This was a good omen, though not of itself sufficient to win me over to the Salvatorians. He ushered me into a very large room which was completely empty of furniture, save for a cheap iron-frame bed, a few wooden chairs and a small table at which a priest was working. His welcoming smile filled the room. I had never seen any man who looked so completely contented; his happiness was all the more moving because of its contrast with the emptiness of the room. He seemed quite unconcerned about the poverty that surrounded him and appeared to be filled with such inner spiritual joy that he won my heart to the Salvatorians. He explained the purpose and ideals of this modern movement and as he spoke he convinced my mind as well as my heart. Much of what he said echoed my own thoughts and ideals and I now saw how right Father Lester had been in suggesting that I should become a Salvatorian. I found myself attracted to them, not by their display of talent, but by their simple poverty. The seeds of my vocation had sprung from the sight of the poverty of the Birmingham slums, and now it was to flower out of the freely accepted poverty of these dedicated men.

The priest insisted that I stay for dinner and we entered the refectory where some fifty students were already assembled. A passage from the Scriptures was read and then permission to talk was given. Immediately a babel of noise broke out; it lapped round me and relaxed me like the warmth of waves on a summer beach. I felt as though I was already a member of a happy family in which no one stood on their dignity and everyone was accepted as a part of the whole.

After dinner I was shown the wooden huts where the students lived and studied and I was deeply impressed by their obvious happiness in spite of these grim living conditions. They came from all parts of the British Isles and from varying home backgrounds, and this diversity made their unity of purpose all the more impressive. I now learned something about the origins and ideals of the Salvatorians.

The Society of the Divine Saviour, now called the Salvatorians, was founded in Rome in 1881 by a young German diocesan priest called Father Francis Jordan. There were points of similarity between his early life and my own that attracted me to him. His mother was also a widow and he was unable to start his studies until he was a man. Being a brilliant linguist, he was sent to Rome to learn Oriental languages; he also spent some time studying in Palestine. While he was in the Holy Land he was inspired to found an active group of learned diocesan priests and laymen who would develop the ideal of the priesthood so as to meet the needs of the times. In fact, he was too far ahead of his times, and it was not until recently that the idea of diocesan priests uniting to form what is now called a secular institute, received official recognition by the Church. In a secular institute, priests and laity unite in a common bond to work for spiritual ideals.

Father Jordan was insistent that his religious family must strive to overcome the limitations of nationality. This is why he made his foundation in Rome, rather than in Germany. He was young and inexperienced in matters of administration and church law, and because of this lack of experience, he was beset with many crises and difficulties. At one time there was an outcry against him because he called his spiritual family the Apostolic Teaching Society. This linking of his name with that of the apostles seemed outrageous to his contemporaries. Out of his vision and crosses his family grew and flourished and it has now spread to all the continents. He was a man born before his time, for his ideals about the priesthood and lay apostles form the keystone of our modern era of salvation history in the Church.

In common with all other spiritual families in the Church, the Salvatorians share the ideal of striving to pattern their lives as closely as is practical on the life of Jesus. To do this means leaving all things behind and following him in poverty, chastity and obedience. It means the living of a celibate life, not from motives of escapism, but in order to strive for more dedicated depths of loving. And just as Christ was obedient until his death, in the same way the practising of intelligent and voluntary obedience is the hallmark of a religious.

These ideals can be stated in a few lines, but their fruitful practice demands a lifelong struggle. Man first fell because he wished to be independent of God.

It was arranged that I should go to the Salvatorian grammar school at Wealdstone and make myself useful there while I completed my studies of Latin. On my return home we began our final preparations for the sale of our livestock. We bought a site at Westington, Chipping Campden, and engaged a local builder to build a stone house for my mother. He was a member of the Guild of Handicraft. This guild, which had started at Toynbee Hall in the East End of London, had been formed by a group of artists and craftsmen, including William Morris, Ruskin, Burne-Jones and C. R. Ashbee. Eventually, some of them decided to move to Chipping Campden and here forty families settled. They took over the old silk mill that had once belonged to members of my mother's family and which had specialized in the making of Parisian silk.

The Guild dissolved itself when it was in danger of becoming too commercialized, but some of its members remained and attracted other craftsmen to this lovely old town. To visit Chipping Campden is to understand why so many artists have lived and worked there. I know of no other town that has such dignity of buildings and whose main street has such grace of outline. Walking down it is like walking down the nave of an old Benedictine abbey. This street is to England what Florence is to Italy, for both reflect the beauties of medieval Europe, and there was, in fact, a close connection between the two towns, for Campden marketed wool in its exquisite old market-hall while Florence provided the finance for its international trade.

My mother wanted a small house and a large garden and

she got her wish. Helping her to make a garden out of a bare field was immensely satisfying, and the months that followed were overflowing with happiness. To be able to create a garden is as rare a privilege as being allowed to build a church. In both cases one is making a hallowed place that will give joy and happiness as the years go by. This garden needed creating, almost literally, as it meant building dry stone walls, rockeries, long winding paths, crazy paving, a sundial and a summer-house. The site was superb and commanded glorious views. The town of Chipping Campden lay at our feet and in the near distance the lofty church tower caught the morning sun, while in the far distance we could see range after range of hills.

We bought a hundred tons of old stone from a farmer friend for making the dry stone walls; this was quite an art. To make a normal-sized wall, one started on an eighteen-inch base and tapered it to about nine inches at the top. The middle had to be kept well filled so that the stone sloped downwards and the rain was diverted outwards. Stone walls give interest to a garden when flowers are out of season.

Building the summer-house was great fun too. I used the remnants of our stock of ash poles for the framework and made the walls out of plaited willows. The roof was thatched with beautiful rushes brought from the mill where our corn used to be ground on the River Stour. They were of a delicate green and changed their shade of colour with every variation of the sunlight. In the summertime I sometimes slept in the summer-house, and it was exhilarating to be woken by the song of birds and to breathe the fragrant scent of flowers still wet from the dew.

Across the valley from our garden was lovely Dover's Hill. This had once been the site of Roman villas, and what a talent the Romans had for picking the beauty spots of England in which to live. Its present name is that of the man who founded the Whitsun Cotswold Games as a protest against the Puritanism of his times. The hill forms a huge natural amphitheatre which now belongs to the National Trust.

Our sale was an enormous success, as many of the dealers who had bought our stock over the years turned up to support us. Our pony Jane had such a reputation for speed in the district that, in spite of her thirteen years, she sold for twice the sum we had paid for her ten years previously. She was a dappled grey and a pretty sight, and the blacksmith, who had shod her over the years, had spent hours in grooming her for the sale. We hated having to sell her and part of my heart went with her.

In the autumn of 1933 I went to the Salvatorian grammar school at Wealdstone. This is on the borders of the Harrow Weald district which was then mostly fields and trees.

The church was designed by Adrian Scott and is very attractive. Inside it is a forest of massive stone arches, and though these obscure the view of the altar, they give a sense of privacy and prayerfulness which must be widely felt for one rarely enters the church without finding someone making their private devotions.

The parish at Wealdstone was a large one and our school had been started some ten years previously as a Catholic grammar school. When I began teaching there we had about a hundred boys. Now there are six hundred. The then headmaster had been ordained at the age of forty-five. He was a lovable character and had the English reserve and gentle form of holiness that reminded me of my old headmaster at Stratford.

Next year I was sent to teach history at the Salvatorian House of Studies at Abbots Langley. Our house there is an old Elizabethan half-timbered building, though it has since been covered with a Georgian façade. The High Street and old flint village church are very charming. Nearby, at Bedmond, is the birthplace of the only English pope, Nicholas Breakspear, who became Pope Adrian IV.

Often I took the enchanting walk through the country lanes to St Albans. Passing the site of the British town of Praed Wood on the left, there is a magnificent view of the ruins of the Roman city of Verulamium in the valley below, while on the opposite side of the valley the hill is dominated by the splendid Norman tower of the abbey and the town of St Albans.

Few spots in England are so soaked in history as this hallowed place where the first martyr in this country, the Roman soldier St Alban, was beheaded. The massive Norman tower is built out of Roman brick taken from the old Roman city ruins and reminded me of the hub of a gaily painted wheel. It is debatable whether this abbey is the most beautiful of our English abbeys, but it is probably the best practical example of the various styles showing the development of architecture among pre-Reformation abbeys.

Chapter 9

THE PROBLEMS OF A NOVICE

ALTHOUGH there are many spiritual families in the Church and they differ considerably in spirit and customs, all share certain basic principles. The origin of religious Orders is an involved and complicated story that is as old as Christianity itself and, indeed, goes back to pre-Christian times, for many of the prophets of the Old Testament were pioneers of this way of life.

But the group of apostles gathered round the Saviour formed the first religious family of the Church. Christ made it a condition that they left all temporal goods behind them in order to follow him in trusting love and obedience. Much of our Lord's public life was spent in training these men to become future spiritual leaders. Part of this training was theoretical, and part consisted in the practical service and instruction of people who were in physical or spiritual need.

The holy women of Nazareth, who followed Christ and ministered to the needs of his disciples, were symbolic of those thousands of holy women who have followed him with love and dedication in religious life through the centuries.

With the conversion of the Roman Empire to Christianity, and the consequent sudden influx of many converts to Christianity, there was a danger that these ideals might be lost, and thus it happened that many holy men and women retired to the deserts of Egypt and Palestine to live the life of hermits – the original word for monk means a hermit.

But before long it became obvious that the life of a hermit

was a rare form of vocation and that the majority of men and women needed the strength and stability of family life to prevent them from developing into cranks. St Benedict was the genius who instituted a stable form of life based on the wholesomeness of family life. The pillars of his success were hard work and unceasing prayer. This simple formula has brought a rich harvest of graces and spiritual treasures which have helped to build up Christian civilization through the centuries.

With the flowering of the early Middle Ages and the spread of town culture, the need arose for men such as the friars who made the world their cloister. Poets, such as St Francis, opened men's eyes to the beauties that surrounded them and showed them how rich contentment can be found in the ideal of simplicity. St Anthony, his disciple, showed them the treasures of the Scriptures.

The scandals and mistakes that caused the tragic break-up of Christianity during the sad time of the Reformation, and the consequent Counter-Reformation, gave birth to a type of religious Order that was to put its emphasis on the office of the priesthood rather than on the ideal of a lay monk. It was St Ignatius's ideal of the priesthood that gave rise to many religious families, each of which had their own spirit and ideals; among them was the one that I now hoped to join.

The Church wisely insists that any young man or woman must undergo a time of probation before becoming a member of a religious family. During this period they have a chance to try out their vocation and are also put to the test by experienced members of the Order.

Nowadays, for various social reasons, we seem to be in danger of exaggerating the age gap between the old and young generations. There has always been some truth in the normal division of interests between the age groups, and there always will be. But there is another side to this which we tend to overlook, and this is the natural love and respect that does exist between the old and the young. Since early times, wisdom has been handed down from generation to generation. This handing-down is the main job of the novice master. The novice willingly puts himself under the guidance of an experienced master, and surely it is interesting that in these sophisticated days a group of young, successful pop-singers should have felt the need to travel to India and there spend some time trying to penetrate the deeper mysteries of life under the guidance of an aged guru.

The noviceship is a time of challenge during which one strives to get to know oneself in depth and thus to seek for a deeper knowledge of the Trinity within. If one can find the courage to be completely honest with oneself, this can at times be a shocking experience. Vague theories of holiness have a nasty way of evaporating at five-thirty on a cold winter's morning.

Our house, Christleton Hall, was situated on the outskirts of Chester. We lived in the converted stables and there was no heating apart from a coke stove on the ground floor which belched smoke when the wind was in the wrong direction. We rose at five-thirty and washed and shaved in cold water. After morning prayers we then spent an hour in mental prayer which was followed by mass and thanksgiving. Afterwards came a breakfast of bread and marmalade on weekdays and bacon on Sundays. It was followed by the recitation, in common, of the divine office of the day. Then we washed up and set out the refectory table for the community's dinner – it numbered fifty at this time. We also did most of the housework. A period of study was followed by a talk from our novice master on the spiritual life and on our rule.

After dinner more washing-up, the recital of the divine office and then a short period of recreation. Twice a week we went for walks or played football during the afternoons, the rest of the time we worked in the garden. In the evening we recited matins and lauds and then did private study. After supper we tidied up the refectory and had another period of relaxation; before we went to bed the master gave us points for next morning's mental prayer. We slept in a dormitory; one of our brothers snored so loudly that we kept a stock of boots by our beds with which to bombard him.

As time went by I found that I was being forced by the exacting circumstances of the daily routine and the irksomeness of my duties to see myself as I really was and to cut out my daydreams.

But this growing insight into myself was only the negative side of this spiritual formation. It was far more difficult to co-operate with God's grace in building up the life of Christ within me. This sounds easy. In practice, it demands Churchillian 'blood, toil, tears and sweat'. It is true that God never refuses graces to those who seek them in good faith, but each of us has to be ready to co-operate with these graces. There are no short-cuts to holiness; there is only the way of deep humility, and this is the hardest way of all.

The ideal towards which we must strive is that our bodies should become the living temples of the Holy Spirit. In part, this is what happens to any soul that is in a state of friendship with God, but the snag is that we so often force God to share our heart with trifles.

During this year of testing we spent most of our day in complete silence, and when talking was allowed it was only to our fellow-novices and to the novice master. In this way we tried to cut ourselves off from the world in order to have time in which to sort ourselves out in the sight of God. I welcomed this chance to seek for God in silence, but there were times when the world clamoured at the door of my heart and would not be denied entry.

We were fortunate in that our novice master was a man of deep and practical spirituality. He had a vivid insight into the mysteries of the life of the soul and was a man of intense prayerfulness. He was typical of a good Salvatorian in that he never abused his authority and he urged us onwards by the telling force of his good example. He could be as gentle as a mother in caring for our spiritual needs and yet, in matters of principle, he was as strong as steel. I owe him a tremendous debt of gratitude, not so much for what he said as for what he was.

One of the novices was a Londoner who had been in the navy. Another was Scottish and had been a professional musician. There was an engineer from Belfast, a printer from Birkenhead, and a dock tally-clerk from Liverpool. Like myself, they were all in their twenties. We were completely different in character and temperament, and as we had to rely on each other for company for a whole year, we were forced to learn to give and take. In the beginning it was easy to get on well together, but as the months went by the tensions grew, small irritations began to rasp, and it took a lot of self-control to keep the peace.

The study and practice of mental prayer formed an important part of our training. Our master was far too wise to force us into any one rigid mould of prayer. He left us free to find our own way of seeking a closer union with God. At times prayer seemed easy and at other times almost impossible. We had to learn by trial and error to be independent of feelings and emotions.

Many of the excellent books on prayer that are available today had not yet been published. The books that I read were written by men trained in scholastic philosophy and they made the mistake of putting too great an emphasis on a detailed analysis of prayer rather than on building up prayer in a constructive manner.

Like most students for the priesthood, I spent much of my time in preaching future sermons for other people rather than for myself. Still, the effort that was necessary in endeavouring to pray for an hour on end did force me to try to explore the depths of prayer within my soul, and this was a genuine help in my seeking for God.

For the most part, my time at Christleton Hall was a very happy one and I was grateful to God for having given me this year to devote entirely to him; it made a solid bridgehead between the past and the future. The greatest trial was the loss of independence. Every moment of our day followed a rigid timetable and we were always at the beck and call of our master. In practice, he left us mostly to our own initiative, but in one's deeper self one felt the loss of freedom and independence. The only occasion on which we handled money was on our one day's outing in the year. We cycled to Liverpool with one shilling and sixpence each. We took sandwiches with us, and as we could not find a park in the centre of the city, we ended up by eating them in a churchyard.

But what a surprise and thrill it was to see the lovely view of Liverpool for the first time from across the width of the River Mersey which, by comparison, makes the Thames look like a mill-stream.

During our afternoon walks we often visited Chester, and its beauty fascinated me every time I saw the city. To stand in one of its famous rows and to look down the main street with its variety of half-timbered shops is as interesting as being on the deck of a sailing-ship. The rows consist of two arcades which run down the entire length of the main streets on both the first floor and the ground floor of the buildings. This type of building is made possible because of the timber framework, but with modern methods of construction, similar arcades would be very practical in our modern shopping centres and would double the shop frontage.

Walking round the city walls was quite an experience. One half expected to be challenged by a Roman sentry, for Chester was an outpost of the Roman Empire and for centuries it was the bulwark against Wales. There is an old law that says that any Welshman found walking in Chester after dark shall be locked up!

The first guide-book ever written in England was compiled in the thirteenth century by a Chester priest. He describes how the tide then lapped the city walls and says that there is no need to go as far as the Indies to hear fabulous tales when such wonders take place daily at the city gates. He tells his visitors that the patron saints of the churches guard the city. Peter, being a fisherman, guards the Water Gate. John, the apostle of light, has charge of the Eastern Gate because it faces the sunrise. Michael guards the South Gate, but the hardest gate of all to guard is the North Gate, because all evil things come from the north and so this gate is left to the care of the town's patroness, St Werburgh. The author's comment is that a woman guards what no man can guard.

Throughout this year of testing, I was to find that my fight for independence was far more deep-seated than I had imagined. One soon learned to obey externally, but to attain the inner spirit of obedience required payment in flesh and blood.

In my *naïveté* I had thought that we would spend most of our time praying in the chapel. I was soon to find out that we had to seek for God with our knees on the cold stone floor of the kitchen with soap-suds on our hands, and this taught me that the hardest work of all is to kneel down and try to pray mentally. The mind darts off at a tangent and thoughts buzz round like flies in the summer heat. There are times when prayer seems easy, though for the most part it is a constant struggle against all sorts of distractions. Dr Robinson, in his *Honest to God*, has a very telling passage in which he describes his personal difficulties in mental prayer. He finds that his prayer seems more fruitful when he is fully engaged on some pastoral problem and that he cannot pray when disengaged. It may be that he comes near to stating a complex problem in the practice of mental prayer, though it is also possible that he over-simplifies things. Ideally speaking, all our activities should engender a spirit of prayer if done with the intention of pleasing God. But if prayer is to become ever more fruitful, it must be nourished by periods of recollection and zones of silence. In religious life, these zones of silence tend, for the sake of convenience, to follow a set pattern at intervals of time, but the time factor is a secondary matter compared to the fact that these zones of silence are there when needed.

In spite of the external frustrations of this year of probation, it was a time of deep inner peace and contentment; like coming home after years of anxious search.

Chapter 10

STUDYING PHILOSOPHY IN ROME

AFTER my noviceship and a further year spent in studies, I went to Rome where I spent two years studying philosophy. I travelled with other students. On our arrival we found the station decked with flags to welcome Mussolini home from his visit to Hitler.

The tram set us down in St Peter's Square at two in the morning; at this time it was still enclosed by buildings and was so lovely that for a moment it seemed to me that we had stepped into fairyland. The gigantic columns of Bernini's colonnade towered high above us, and the dome of St Peter's floated in the clouds like a huge balloon. The soft moonlight glowed warmly on the golden travertine stone and reminded me of the Cotswolds. On either side of the square the twin fountains flung their sparkling sprays into the skies with careless abandonment, and as the waters fell they made music. I lost my heart to these fountains; none can compare with them.

The big outer doors of our motherhouse were locked for the night and we knocked on them in vain. We searched around until we saw a lighted doorway which turned out to be the local police station. Three sleepy policemen looked at us in astonishment as we explained our predicament by gesture; eventually we persuaded them to telephone our house. There was no reply, so they kindly came round with us and hammered on the door with their truncheons. Still there was no response. A few drops of rain began to fall and with every drop the policemen's courage proceeded to evaporate till, with a polite shrug of their shoulders, they left us to our fate. After some time we decided that the only thing to do was to let out a piercing whistle, even if it meant waking the Pope on the opposite side of the piazza. At this a head popped out of an upper window and not long afterwards we were fast asleep in snow-white sheets.

Our motherhouse is an historic old building; it stands opposite St Peter's in an area known as the Borgo. This name originates in the Saxon word for a town, or borough, and, indeed, it was the Saxon kings who established a hostel here for pilgrims visiting Peter's tomb.

Before the war, Rome was as quiet and peaceful as a country village. Few people could afford cars and the noisy scooter had not yet been invented. The Italians love noise, but Mussolini had strictly enforced rules that forbade the blowing of horns. Nowadays, the city's quiet is ruined by the ceaseless noise of traffic, the more so because Romans take a delight in revving up their engines in low gear and driving as though they are on a racing-track.

Each of the great cities of the world has an atmosphere that is undefinable but tangible to a sensitive touch. London has a strong sense of history; Paris is the city of elegance. New York has its village streets and thronged pavements through which people from skyscrapers scurry like ants out of ant-hills. Washington is a monument to the nineteenth century; Athens has its silk-spun air, while Florence is a museum of frozen medieval beauty. Rome cannot be captured in any of these categories for she contains them all, as well as many others. Warm, kindly, homely and intensely human, she is the mother of all fair cities. Each person visiting Rome sees in her the reflection of their own dreams. And herein lies the secret of her motherliness. If one may see Naples and die, then one should see Rome and live. No wonder there are legends about throwing coins in a fountain to ensure one's return, but there is no need of this to feel an intense desire to return.

G. K. Chesterton thought of Rome as the city of the eternal resurrection. There is much truth in this, for Rome is intensely alive, a city of the past, the present and the future. The best of each century cluster together in haphazard spontaneity. Besides being the mother of the Western world, Rome is the eternal woman, full of mystery and surprises. She is also the only city where one never feels alone for Roman streets have a warmth and friendliness which make one feel immediately at home. Apart from the Corso thoroughfares, which were built for horse-racing through the city, most of her streets are very narrow and wind like serpents; they were built like this to keep out the cold winds of winter and to provide shade in the summer heat.

The Romans are a nation of flat-dwellers, and in the poorer quarters they hang out their washing across the street from window to window, which gives a gay and festive appearance. Usually the ground floors are reserved for shops, small businesses and crafts. The shopkeepers sit outside until the late hours of the evening while their children play around them. Everywhere there is laughter and smiles which make one feel part of the family. There is no need of shop-signs, for each shop advertises itself by its pungent aroma. To see Romans sitting around and talking to their friends is like watching the old silent films. Often their gestures are more expressive than their words. But, in spite of the impression of leisure, Italians are very hard-working people and spend long hours at the family business.

It is not difficult for me to recapture the thrill of my first walk across Rome from our motherhouse near St Peter's to the Gregorian University. Although I made this journey nearly every day for two years before the war, and then for another two years after the war, there were always new things to discover.

As we walked along, small children tugged at our long cloaks and begged for holy pictures. Sometimes a group would hang on until we gave them some pictures. They collected them much as English children were then collecting cigarette-cards. When our wide soup-plate hats blew off in the breeze, the children would scream with delight and chase after them with yells of excitement. Italians idolize all children, and Roman children are very attractive, for although they are well behaved, they have no shyness in making friends with anyone.

Nearly every street corner we passed had its shoe-black, for Romans have an obsession for highly polished shoes. Policemen patrolled in pairs, wearing gorgeous blue uniforms with red-braided, cocked hats and tall plumes, and one expected them to burst out into operatic song at any moment. Middle-aged women walked along the pavements, gracefully balancing huge bundles on their heads; men trundled three-wheeled cycles that pulled all sorts of loads; a boy would come flying round a corner on a cycle balancing a tray of cakes on his head, while bricklayers, working on new buildings and wearing hats made out of newspapers, vied with each other as they filled the air with the refrain from an aria.

As we walked through the narrow streets we would suddenly emerge into a peaceful little square. Some of them had exquisitely carved fountains, while others had attractive wall-shrines to our Lady. Every street seemed to have its own church, many of them looking like private houses.

One day, while we were passing the church of St Ignatius, two motorists came speeding round the corner and bumped into each other. Little damage was done, for Roman drivers have very quick reactions. (They need to if they are to survive.) Each driver jumped out of his car and they faced up to each other like fighting-cocks. A lot of shouting and flailing of arms followed, but just when we thought it might be necessary to call the police to prevent murder, they suddenly shook hands, kissed each other on the cheeks as old friends, jumped into their cars and shot off as though it were all a huge joke.

If you should wish to see the Catholic Church in action, by all means visit the Pope, or attend some large ceremony in St Peter's. But if you want to see the full vigour of the Church, then stroll along to the Piazza Pilotta, either at eight in the morning or at midday, for at these hours some three thousand students converge on the Gregorian University. Men from every corner of the globe; fat clerics and thin clerics; men of every possible shade of colour – white, tan, yellow, black; clerics with the shaven heads of the tonsure, and long-haired Greeks, each dressed in the colours of their national colleges or wearing many varieties of religious habit. Here are people of every type of culture and political creed, men differing in every aspect, yet all in agreement on the fundamental truths of their faith; an eloquent witness to the universality of the Catholic Church.

It was good fun to try to spot the various nationalities from their walk. Englishmen loped along like hares. Americans slouched and sauntered as though they owned the universe. Italians took short steps like ballet-dancers.

Germans marched as though on parade. Dutchmen waddled like the fat ducks of their marshes. Spaniards strutted as if fighting a duel. Chinese trotted with deferential steps as though crossing over one of the delightful bridges of a willow-patterned plate. Africans glided as though they were stalking big game. Frenchmen rushed as though catching a train. Indians and Sinhalese did not so much walk as dance along with all the grace of their race.

Entering our huge lecture hall in the university was like being parachuted into Babel. It was tantalizing, and almost frightening, to hear so many languages being spoken all at once and, apart from an occasional English voice, not to be able to understand them. There were one hundred and forty different nationalities at the Gregorian, and it came as a shock to realize how many different nationalities and languages there are in the world. The mind can accept this truth in an abstract way, but to be suddenly thrown into the jumble of sound bewilders the senses.

The essential need to have a common language for teaching such a mixed group now became clear to me. In lieu of a common world language, the Church had solved this problem by making use of what is termed dog-Latin. Classical scholars may turn up their noses at it, but they forget that some such type of spoken language has always been used in the practical affairs of mankind. Our Lord used the popular Aramaic of his day, and the writers of the Gospels used the common form of Greek.

Learning modern languages was one of the advantages of studying in Rome. One teamed up with a Frenchman, a German or an Italian and spoke their language on one day and English on the next day. There were fourteen different nationalities studying at our motherhouse, so we had several languages to choose from.

When I had to see the prefect of our year, he and I did our best to carry on a conversation in halting Latin until I discovered that he was an American. Most of my friends at the Gregorian were Americans. I liked their lack of snobbery and their dynamic outlook, and they had a directness of approach that reminded me of the early Christians.

We were fortunate in the fact that this university was the apple of the eye of the then Father General of the Jesuits. As soon as any Jesuit became outstanding as a professor in any part of the world he was called back to Rome and taught at the Gregorian. It was interesting to note the different approaches of the various nationalities. English professors were practical and precise, but the continentals had great difficulty in understanding the clipped vowels of their pronunciation of Latin. Our German teachers were extremely thorough, though they tended to get lost in a mass of detail. Italians did not so much lecture as preach an eloquent sermon. Belgian dons had brilliant powers of abstraction but easily got lost in the clouds. The Dutch lectured as though they were selling fish in the market, though they were very practical and good teachers. One of our French lecturers was such a good teacher that students would cut other lectures and gate-crash our course in order to hear him. It was a mind-broadening experience to see the way these men of varying nationalities tackled the same basic problems. They were patient and genuinely humble, and this made a deep impression on me. I learned much from them besides philosophy. But philosophy opened up my way to the answers to some of the problems that had puzzled me. Any system of philosophical thought, being of its nature a man-made exercise of human reason, cannot reach out beyond the confines of human reason, but now I saw that religious faith, though at times going out beyond the limits of human understanding in its deeper mysteries, is nevertheless firmly based upon reason and can never contradict reason.

It was a great joy to be introduced to the timeless wisdom of the Greeks and to the width of mind of such thinkers as St Augustine and St Thomas Aquinas. Apart from the subject-matter of our lectures we learned a great deal from having contact with trained minds. It was not only what lecturers said, but also the way they said it that was important.

Several of my fellow-students were later to become pioneers of the thought underlying the Vatican Council, but the initial credit should be given to these able teachers. They taught us to be fearless in our search for truth and to be prepared to follow it, no matter where it might lead. They had a breadth of charity and wisdom which made them recognize the truth in any man's thought. Truth is not the exclusive property of the Catholic Church, even if she is guided by the spirit of truth; indeed, truth may sometimes be quarried in the most unlikely places. The study of the development of philosophy through the ages opened up my mind to the universality and richness of truth and to the thrill of its pursuit.

Chapter 11

A SALVATORIAN IN ST PETER'S

NO ONE can understand why Rome is an eternal city unless he realizes that it is built upon the rock of Peter. Just as its superb dome links and co-ordinates the myriad other churches and buildings of Rome, so does the rock of Peter link and co-ordinate all that is best in Christian thought. Throughout the centuries of Christianity inspiration has flowed from this rock of truth and it has returned to her enriched by the thought of other nations and cultures.

The basilica of St Peter's aptly symbolizes the unity and diversity of the rock of truth. Thackeray complained that whereas the aim of most architects is to make buildings look three times bigger than their real size, this vast church looks three times smaller than it really is. In this way it is typical of the humility of truth. Although I visited St Peter's almost daily for over four years, I continued to discover new treasures. The head sacristan once told me that he had served in the basilica for sixty years but could even today still come upon new things.

We Salvatorians have a special connection with St Peter's, being in charge of the Blessed Sacrament Chapel. The Blessed Sacrament is the real treasure of St Peter's. Take it away and the building would be no more than a museum. From seven in the morning until midday some of us were on duty there, giving Holy Communion to the constant stream of pilgrims. We also had care of the baptistry. All Romans are free to have their children christened there, and twice a week about sixty are baptized during the day.

The best time to see St Peter's is when it is completely empty. Many times I have walked through the basilica from the sacristy entrance to prepare for early morning mass in the Blessed Sacrament Chapel before it is opened to the public. At this hour the vast expanses do not overwhelm or dwarf but offer warmth and protection, and there is a wonderful and deep peace and tranquillity. But even when St Peter's is crowded with pilgrims it is still a house of prayer and it is so big that it is always possible to find quiet corners. Often there is a sung mass going on in one part of the building, a sermon being preached in another part, babies yelling their heads off in the baptistry, groups of pilgrims being shown round by guides, and yet one can still kneel in the Blessed Sacrament Chapel and hear nothing of it.

To attend any papal function in the basilica is to enter into a dreamworld of pageantry and colour. Nowadays, the tendency is to replace this elaborate ceremonial with austere simplicity which is considered more fitted to the mood of our generation. While one can sympathize with this desire, one must also admit that there is much that pleases the eye that is going to be lost in the process. A lot of the child remains in the man; there is a delight in dressing up for special occasions and, after all, this is often one of the supreme moments in the life of many of the pilgrims, and surely such moments merit special treatment?

During a beatification ceremony the Pope gives the benediction, and as we have the sole charge of the Blessed Sacrament Chapel, it is our privilege to assist him at this service.

The funeral of Pius XI was one of the most touching of these ceremonies. The day he died there was a continuous stream of cardinals, bishops and diplomats calling to pay their respects. Towards evening the general public was allowed to pass by the body laid out in the Sistine Chapel. I was at the head of the queue of thousands of people pushing, as only Romans can push. After a time the pressure was so great that it was impossible to move in any direction and I was in danger of being crushed to death against the stone pillars of Bernini's colonnade. Police, firemen and soldiers were rushed in to try to keep the crowds in check. After three hours of this increasing pressure something seemed to snap and I and an Italian businessman were catapulted, like corks out of a champagne bottle, through the barrier of soldiers and firemen standing twenty deep. It was rather as if we were birds soaring in the breeze and we both landed unhurt after a flight of about fifty feet. The ranks closed behind us and we shook hands in congratulation and made our way unhindered to the Sistine Chapel. It was dusk as we entered and the only light was that of flickering candles that surrounded the bier. Four of the Noble Guard were on duty, otherwise the chapel was empty, save for two old ladies from the Pope's domestic staff who were kneeling by the body saying their rosaries. We knelt and joined them in prayer.

As my eyes became accustomed to the soft light I realized that we were kneeling opposite Michelangelo's *Last Judgment*, and what a perfect setting it made for the majestic scene of a Pope's lying-in-state. Pope or peasant, all are at one in the awesome presence of death and all must answer the same important questions. Tears were streaming down the cheeks of the two old servants and they could easily have been peasant women mourning the death of a son.

For a time Pius XI was buried in the crypt. Then, when the war broke out, it was decided to place the tomb in an alcove. It was while doing this that the workmen found a hollow niche in the wall. Monsignor Kaas, the former head of the German Centre Party who had been exiled by Hitler, was in charge of the fabric of St Peter's. As there were not so many pilgrims owing to the war, he thought it an opportune time to close the crypt and make a thorough investigation of the whole area under the basilica. This marked the beginning of the excavation work that led to the discovery of the street and catacombs upon which Constantine had built the original church. It also led to the finding of what seems to be St Peter's tomb.

Chapter 12

EUROPE ON THE EVE OF WAR

EVER since the return of Mussolini from his visit to Hitler, which took place on the day of my arrival in Rome, there had been growing tension in Italy. Large placards were erected in the Forum depicting the growth of the old Roman Empire and a significant empty place was left for Mussolini's new empire-to-be.

By tradition, there had always been friendly relations between England and Italy, but the sanctions that were imposed after Italy's cowardly attack on Abyssinia gave Mussolini the excuse that he was looking for in order to help sway public opinion towards friendship with Hitler. The Italians are a peace-loving people; now many of them were afraid they would get dragged, against their will, into a war just to satisfy the dream of this proud man.

Every few weeks Mussolini would harangue the crowd from the balcony of his headquarters in the Venetian Square and try to stir them into the same mass hysteria as Hitler was raising in Germany. It seems incredible that the English politicians of those days were unable to read the signs of the times when, to anyone living in Rome, war and the threat of war was a constant theme.

This propaganda built up into an elaborate climax with Hitler's visit to Rome. Extraordinary precautions were taken to ensure his safety. Some six months before he arrived we were relaxing on the flat roof of our motherhouse when we noticed that the small rooms of a nearby hotel were crammed full with a dozen beds per room. Afterwards we discovered that these were for the German secret police, of whom several thousand were stationed in Rome during Hitler's stay.

A temporary station was built to receive him so that he could enter Rome along the old triumphant route leading to the Forum. Pope Pius XI showed his disapproval by moving out to Castel Gandolfo and speaking out bluntly about the broken cross of the swastika being the sign of the times.

For the first three days of the visit the centre of Rome was taken over by the secret police; it was ringed round with soldiers, and no one was allowed to enter this area unless they had a pass signed by the Fascists or the Nazis.

Two of us went to try to see Hitler, but we found that the soldiers had blockaded all the roads some distance from where he was likely to appear. There was no chance of bluffing our way through where the Germans were on duty, so we searched around until we found a street where only Italian soldiers were on guard. We had nothing to show them except our English passports, but as these were obviously official-looking documents, the officer in charge let us through.

As the ranks closed behind us we felt a sudden panic, for if we were now challenged by the secret police we would be in serious trouble. Fortunately for us, there was no need to worry, for we entered into a world that seemed like a scene from a comic opera. Italian and German officials and officers were strutting around, shouting instructions, and were far too busy trying to impress each other to take any notice of two clerics. I thought how easy it would have been for an assassin to have dressed up as a priest and concealed a gun under the long clerical coat.

In the end, Hitler and Mussolini passed within six feet of

where we had posted ourselves. They were both standing up in an open car surrounded by bullet-proof glass, and one could see the fear of assassination reflected in their grim faces. Later, during the visit, a soldier did shoot at them. This happened in a side street and was witnessed by an American friend of mine, but it was hushed up.

The first thing that struck me about Hitler was that he looked so very ordinary. He had high cheek bones and a fresh complexion, and when in repose his face looked friendly; in fact, he reminded me of an uncle of mine. The only outstanding thing about him were his eyes; these were extraordinary in their brilliance and intensity. They flashed with the inner fire of a man who believes that he is inspired. They were deep violet in colour and of that rare type that turns black under the stress of emotion. His eyes explain his remarkable hold over people.

There was no cheering and one had a sense of foreboding, as though the hand of death was on these two men, but little did we then realize just how much death and suffering they would bring to Europe.

Our Father General now decided to send us to visit some of our colleges in Germany and Austria during the summer holidays, as it seemed only a matter of time before we lost them to the Nazis. The first one we stayed at was in a small town in Swabia. When out walking with a German student, I happened to say something about the Nazis; at once he hushed me into silence and when we got home he explained that some three hundred people out of this small town had already disappeared for speaking against the Nazis. Unless one has lived in a police-state one cannot understand how frustrated and powerless ordinary people become under a tyranny.

During our travels we found the German people very friendly and hospitable and most of them were just as frightened as we were that the Nazis were going to plunge Europe into war. It was pathetic to see how much confidence they had in England's power to prevent this happening.

There was a large farm attached to the college and they had a first-class team of lay brothers who not only looked after it but were also trained builders, carpenters, gardeners, mechanics and tailors. Each man was a master of his craft and together they lived a life of intense activity and prayerfulness and were an example to us all. They had a simple and solid type of piety that was most attractive. Dedicated men such as this are the salt of the earth.

A group of us reached Munich on the very day that Chamberlain arrived on his famous peace mission. We did not know about this and were very surprised to see the station bedecked with Union Jacks. We were wearing our religious habits which so scared the young priest who came to meet us that he pushed us into the nearest tram, even though it was going in the wrong direction, explaining that groups of clerics were likely to be arrested.

When we arrived at our college they dressed us in civilian clothes as a safety measure. These clothes had been handed in for a jumble-sale; some fitted, others did not, and we looked a motley crowd. It was a small incident but enough to open my eyes to the terror of a police-state.

The next of our colleges we visited was at Passau on the banks of the Danube by the Austrian border. Passau is one of the loveliest towns in Europe and the setting is beautiful for three rivers meet here and flow into the Danube. The college is situated high up on the hills and the views from its windows are awe-inspiring, especially in the late evening, when the lights are reflected in the dancing ripples of the river below.

The days that followed were the anxious ones of the Munich crisis. Soldiers, guns and mules were constantly crossing the Passau bridge to take up positions near the Sudeten border. The bishop loaned us his car to visit a beauty spot near the border, but as he needed it in the evening we returned home by a train which was crammed with Sudeten refugees. A hundred soldiers were billeted at our college and they had no idea how serious the crisis really was. Most of these soldiers were men of our own age who had been drafted for military service and hated the idea of war as much as we did.

It was by now far too dangerous for us to stay in Germany, so we started on our return journey to Rome. One of our students had friends at the Jesuit college at Innsbruck who invited us for supper there. When we arrived we found the front windows smashed in and fire-hoses lying along the passages. The rector told us that the night before they had been raided by a gang of Nazi hooligans. Now the fire-hoses were going to be manned at night by the seventy English and American students.

We left Rome just before the outbreak of the war. An Italian who, as a youth, had worked alongside Mussolini, was in our compartment. He told us that he belonged to an anti-Fascist movement based in France. It was a frightening experience to witness his wife's terror when we came to the border where we did our best to divert attention from her by joking with the guards. When we reached England, it shocked us to see how complaisant the majority of people were, and how sure they seemed that war was an impossibility.

Chapter 13

HEYTHROP THEN AND NOW

OUR Father General would have liked me to return to Rome to complete my studies in theology, but the war made this impossible. The only place in England where one could then study for a degree in Catholic theology was the Jesuit college at Heythrop in Oxfordshire. This college did not at that time take non-Jesuit students, but in the exceptional circumstances they accepted me. The Jesuits were extremely kind and helpful, and as our province was very poor and my mother was paying my fees, they took me in at a very reduced rate.

The older part of the college had been built in the eighteenth century by the Earl of Shrewsbury. After being gutted by fire it was restored by Thomas Brassey, a man who had made a fortune building railways in various parts of the world. Its architecture misses what is best in the Cotswold tradition, but the park, consisting of woods, lakes, hills and valleys, and designed by Capability Brown, is very lovely. It has a fine variety of trees which look their best in spring and autumn when the contrasting shades of their leaves change every few days.

The Jesuits, owing to the major part they played during the Counter-Reformation, are often misjudged. Having lived with them over a period of four years, I can only speak of them with the highest praise. The simplicity of their lives, their tremendous capacity for hard work and their complete dedication to the service of others, stand out very clearly.

They are individualists, in the best sense of the word, and show great courage in tackling tough assignments. They have a deep sense of loyalty, not only towards the Church, but also towards each other.

I found that learned men such as Henry Davis, the moral theologian, and Edmund Sutcliffe, the biblical scholar, were as simple as children in their manner of life. Father Sutcliffe used to cycle the six miles to Chipping Norton most afternoons to work in the nuns' garden there. Father Joyce, the convert son of a former vicar of Harrow, had a mind that was devastatingly clear and brilliant and he was the terror of the oral examination board. Shortly after I was ordained I was privileged to give him Holy Communion on the day before he died – he was then over eighty. His simple devotion and childlike faith were most impressive. Men such as these are the salt of the earth and give a joy and a zest to life.

Although the majority of the professors were excellent teachers, the text-book method then in vogue left much to be desired. There was too much dead-wood and needless repetition of insignificant detail. Much of this could have been eliminated and it would have been better to have concentrated on fewer and more basic problems and to have treated them in greater depth. There could also have been more integration of our various courses, so that the same question would have been dealt with at the same time from the varying aspects of the specialized subjects. Since those days the method of teaching theology has greatly improved and the Jesuits have been in the forefront of this reform.

It was during my years at Heythrop that the idea of the various religious Orders in England uniting to form a common centre of studies came into my mind. There was nothing new in this, for the universities of Oxford and Cambridge owe their origin to a similar grouping of religious Orders. I thought that this centre of studies could well be at Heythrop since it was sixteen miles from Oxford. Technically it was outside the university boundaries, but it did not seem too improbable that, with goodwill, an exception might be made. The Jesuits had the immense advantage of possessing one of the world's finest theological libraries in the English language and, in some ways, an adequate library seemed to me even more important to this type of centre than its staff, for while the religious Orders could combine to form a well-qualified teaching staff, it would take generations to build up a library such as that which the Jesuits already possessed.

There were at that time between twenty and thirty seminaries for religious study in England. A few of them were sufficiently big to justify the services of a large and qualified teaching staff, but the majority were so small that it was a waste of manpower to staff them. Too small a grouping of students meant that they often lacked some things essential to their training and it also tended to make them narrow and self-enclosed. Even in a community of nearly two hundred, as at Heythrop, there was still a danger of the group becoming too self-enclosed. Newman has pointed out that a university training should consist not so much in memorizing a mass of facts and figures, as in an exchange of ideas between thinking minds.

When I was at the Gregorian University, half the students were religious and half were diocesan students, and I found this contact with diocesans very beneficial. I therefore believed that it would be good if some of the diocesan students were to study at the centre if ever it came into being, for this would help towards a more efficient working partnership and understanding between secular priests and religious. It was also evident that much needed to be done to help nuns and lay teachers of religion to become more qualified. A centre of theology would make it possible for them to take their degrees in theology.

At that time any priest who wished to take a degree in Catholic theology or philosophy could only do so on the continent. I was convinced that while it was good that some English priests should study abroad, we also needed a centre of Catholic theology in England where Englishmen could develop their native talents.

I often talked with several of my fellow-students about the possibility of opening up Heythrop to outsiders. The majority were in favour of the plan though they thought it would be some years before it could be initiated. In fact, nothing came of the idea until 1959. During that year we Salvatorians decided to close down our seminary at Chester and take practical steps towards starting a centre of higher studies along with other religious. It seemed to us to be imperative to enlist the help of the Jesuits in the forming of this centre, and since they were not willing to leave Heythrop, where they were planning to build a large and modern library, it was decided that the centre should be based on Heythrop. The English hierarchy were approached and they gave their full support to the idea. One of the last acts of Cardinal Godfrey was to obtain permission from Rome for the granting of degrees for non-Jesuits at Heythrop.

Then came the Second Vatican Council and the new outlook on the training of priests, and this meant that the future of the Heythrop project was assured, for nuns and laity were now included in the scheme. A dozen religious Orders made plans for building halls of residence in the park. We Salvatorians built ours there and were followed by the De Montfort fathers and the Holy Child nuns. Several other religious who had houses in the area joined in, while others sent their students as boarders. Then came the credit squeeze and many religious Orders that had planned to build at Heythrop found themselves unable to borrow sufficient money for this purpose.

All the same, these were years of pioneering and experimenting and they were invaluable to the success of the Heythrop project, for we proved beyond doubt that students from different religious families and traditions could work and study along with nuns and lay people to the advantage of everybody concerned. When the idea of a study centre was first debated among the major superiors of the religious Orders, there were some who were afraid that it might lead to a weakening of what was best in the traditions and spirit of their religious families. Our experience has now proved that the exact opposite takes place: spiritual family ties are not weakened but enriched by contacts with outsiders.

Imbued with the spirit of the Second Vatican Council, two movements now began to influence the formation of future priests; the first was the emphasis laid on a more pastoral and practical form of training; the second, a deeper understanding of the implications of the ecumenical movement. The latter caused Heythrop to become a centre of this ecumenical movement. A logical consequence of these two impulses was that the whole Heythrop project should be moved to London where there would be greater opportunities for pastoral work and a more direct contact with non-Catholics. Today Heythrop has been recognized by London University, and this closer contact with university life will bring great benefits to Catholic theology in this country.

Chapter 14

PRAYER AND ORDINATION

LOOKING back on the ten years that I spent in preparation for my ordination the one thing that stands out in my mind is that it is essential that before a man is ordained he should become a man of prayer; he must love prayer and have a genuine and humble appreciation of its importance in his life. If he lacks this, then his life as a priest will be sterile. People turn to him for help not so much because of his theoretical knowledge as because they trust him as a man of prayer.

And yet of all arts known to man that of prayer is the most elusive and difficult to acquire.

It took me several years to realize that prayer is not so much a science that conforms to set patterns and theories as a craft that needs to be practised if one is to understand it in depth. It is a living and not a static reality and therefore it has as many facets and mysteries as life itself. What suits us at one time in our lives may not suit us at another.

Provided that we are in a state of grace, prayer, in the wider sense of the word, includes all that we do in our daily routine. The Ignatian dictum that all we do should be done for God's honour and glory is but another way of expressing St Paul's teaching that everything we do should be a prayer. St Benedict made a similar point when he said that to work was to pray. Work and prayer if rightly understood and performed with a good intention and a loving heart are closely associated. For most of us to do our duty in our own state of life is our main form of prayer.

Nevertheless, it is true also that if we are to perform our work with the intention of pleasing God then we need some periods of recollection and silence during our day's activities.

Mental prayer can look very complicated when it is analysed on paper, and some of the books written about it may scare lay people off the idea of attempting to practise it. But the simple fact is that most good people use some form of mental prayer every day of their lives even if they are unaware of doing so. Each time they raise their thoughts to God they are praying.

There is a vast difference between the Englishman's approach to prayer and that of the Latin mind. The latter tend towards flamboyance and superlatives whereas we prefer a more simple and direct approach to God. As there is a part of prayer which is really a conversation between the soul and God it follows that people will often pray in the manner in which they talk. English people may have a wide vocabulary for their written language, but in their spoken language they are usually terse and direct.

Prayer is a dialogue between the soul and God and therefore concerns two parties and, as in human friendship, they may not always feel in the mood for talking. Shared silence can be even more full of depth than the spoken word.

The curse of our modern civilization is loneliness. Loneliness can eat into our souls and make us feel unknown and unwanted in this noisy world of rush and restlessness. We all need a strong sense of security and of belonging. Deep down within us we need an understanding friend who loves us with an enduring love. The splendour of the life of prayer means that we find therein a friend who never fails us in our need. The man of prayer is a happy man and he is never alone. This is why such men are towers of strength to those who feel lost and lonely amid the strains and tensions of modern life. Modern men tend to become remote islands. Prayer must be the bridge between them.

My ordination took place in 1943. It came as the fulfilment of half a lifetime. It brought a sense of deep peace and inner contentment. It was as though time stood still and one had a glimpse of eternity.

Arriving at Wealdstone the night before my ordination, I found the then superior, a man whose heart was as big as his boots, and the rest of the community on their knees scrubbing and polishing the floor of one of the classrooms that was to serve as a temporary refectory. This was typical of all that is best in community life.

The Adrian Scott church made a lovely setting for an ordination, the first in Harrow since the Reformation. Lying prostrate on the altar steps during the singing of the litanies my whole life flashed before me. Every step of the journey had given me a widening and an enriching of my known world. Babyhood at the foot of a Cotswold hill, boyhood at the Old Wharf, schooldays at Stratford-on-Avon, apprenticeship in Birmingham, noviceship at Chester, philosophy in Rome, theology at Heythrop. Each step had been a move into a new form of existence.

This growth had been twofold, outwards and inwards. My efforts at mental prayer had taught me that God's Kingdom is to be found within, yet the paradox is that the deeper the insight into this inner reality the greater the urge to help those who are outside this inner sanctuary of love. There can be no genuine love of God without a parallel love of one's neighbour. My main job as a priest would be to build bridges between God and men.

During the ordination the newly ordained priest concelebrates mass with the bishop, and this is his first mass. The chalice standing on the altar is the only thing that is visible to the laity during the mass. A chalice aptly sums up the life and work of a priest. Day after day in the mass the fruits of man's labour in the form of bread and wine are liturgically offered up by the priest as an act of thanksgiving and sacrifice to God their creator. God accepts these gifts and through the mystery of his love changes them into the living reality of himself as man's spiritual food. This is indeed a great mystery and it is only the mystery of love that can make any sense of it, for why should an almighty Being be bothered with fickle creatures unless love be the driving force?

In the spiritual life of the sacraments God makes use of the simple but basic realities of life, wine, bread, water and oil, to act as links between man and God.

The next morning I said mass for my mother and the sisters at the Salvatorian convent chapel at Abbots Langley. We then went to Chester where I was to sing my first solemn mass.

During my ordination holiday I said mass in the village where I was born and also at Stratford-on-Avon. I had supper with my old headmaster and he was delighted that I had become a priest, and keenly interested in my life as a religious. I next said mass at Chipping Campden.

My holiday was cut short by an urgent call for help from a busy dockside parish in Liverpool. This area had been badly bombed and the streets were drab and ugly, in sharp contrast to the beauty of the Cotswolds. But it was in this large parish that I was to have my first taste of the fruits of the priesthood. My first experience in hearing confessions was a four-hour, non-stop spell on a Saturday night. I came out of the confessional a very happy man as I realized as never before how many good people there are in the world, and that not a few of these are leading lives of intense and unseen holiness. Beautiful scenery and buildings have their value in an ideal form of existence, but of far greater value is the beauty of a person's inner life, and this can flourish even in the midst of drabness. My job as a priest would be to nurture and encourage this inner growth of beauty.